Clip Notes

for church bulletins

Volume 1
Compiled & edited
by Kathy Luty &
David Philippart

LTP
LITURGY
TRAINING
PUBLICATIONS

Copyright © 1997 Archdiocese of
Chicago: Liturgy Training
Publications, 1800 North Hermitage
Avenue, Chicago IL 60622-1101;
1-800-933-1800, fax 1-800-
933-7094, e-mail orders@ltp.org.
All rights reserved.

This book was edited by Kathy
Luty and David Philippart. M. Urgo
designed it. Audrey Novak Riley
was the production editor. Karen
Mitchell set the type in Helvetica and
Usherwood. *Clip Notes for Church
Bulletins* was printed and bound by
Printing Arts LithoTech, Inc., in
Cicero, Illinois.

Library of Congress Cataloging-in-
Publication Data

Clip notes for church bulletins /
    edited by Kathy Luty and David
    Philippart.
        p.   cm.
    ISBN 1-56854-169-4 (v. 1)
    1. Catholic Church — Equipment
and supplies. 2. Church bulletins.
3. Clip art. 4. Copy art. 5. Church
year. I. Luty, Kathy. II. Philippart,
David.
BX1945.C55   1997
254' .3 — dc21   97-30052
                        CIP

ISBN 1-56854-169-4
NOTES1

Table of Contents

How to Use This Book

Initiation

Sunday Eucharist

Seasons of the Year

Holy Days and Saints' Days

Other Rites

Environment and Art

Suggested Schedule
Sunday by Sunday

Record of Use Chart

How to Use This Book

Here are 75 articles on various aspects of the liturgy, grouped into categories for convenience. The articles do not necessarily make up a comprehensive curriculum on the topic, although the sections on Initiation and Seasons come close. Subsequent volumes of *Clip Notes* will provide more.

You may use these articles in a variety of ways. You might run a topical series of articles for four or five weeks in a row as the need arises, or you might decide to use pieces here and there. Or Sunday by Sunday through the year, you simply may chose to include one article that seems timely. The "Suggested Schedule Sunday by Sunday" at the end of the book suggests ways to use one article a week beginning with the First Sunday of Advent in any year. In some weeks, there are two or three articles to choose from.

The "Record of Use Chart" at the back of the book helps you keep track of how you have used the articles. This will help you remember if you already put a particular article in the Sunday bulletin, or in the school or religious education newsletter, for example.

No page numbers appear on the actual articles, so the copies you make will be neat. Page numbers are on the facing blank page. The back of each article is blank so nothing will show through when you make photocopies. You may scan the article and its art directly into your bulletin, using the disk or your computer's scanner. You may also retype the text into whatever format you'd like. In any case, the copyright notice must always appear as written with the text and art.

You may copy the text and art in this book for your parish, school or institution provided that you are not selling the publication in which it appears. If you are selling the publication, you must write for permission. There may be a fee. In your letter, state exactly which articles and art you wish to copy, how many copies you will make and what you will charge per copy, and the purpose of the publication the articles and art will appear in. Please allow at least one month for a reply. Write or fax: Reprint Permissions, Liturgy Training Publications, 1800 North Hermitage Avenue, Chicago IL 60622-1101; fax: 773-486-7094.

We would be happy to hear your suggestions for future volumes of *Clip Notes*. Write or fax the editor of *Clip Notes* at the same address.

More art is available in Liturgy Training Publications' series of clip art books: *Clip Art for Year A, Clip Art for Year B* and *Clip Art for Year C*. (These are also available on disk.) One new bulletin article and illustration is published in each issue of *Liturgy 90* magazine, published eight times a year. To order, call 1-800-933-1800, fax 1-800-933-7094, e-mail orders@ltp.org.

1

Q&A: Who's Who

Who are the catechumens we hear so much about in church?

Trying to figuring out who's who is a common human activity. At weddings, funerals, family and class reunions we like to know who we are sharing our time with and what relationship they have — or don't have — to us. So it is with the church that gathers on Sunday for Mass. Many of the faces are as familiar as our own, but as with any healthy group, new faces are to be expected and welcomed. Some may be visitors, some may be fellow Catholics who have recently moved into the neighborhood, and some may be responding to a faint or fiery call to find out more about Christ and his church. The church opens its arms to these seekers with the wisdom and rituals of the Rite of Christian Initiation of Adults (commonly called the RCIA).

People who are seeking to learn more about the Catholic faith and its mission fall into two main groups: catechumens and candidates. (*Catechumen* is a strange word. It comes from a Greek word meaning "to resound." The words *catechist* and *catechism* are related to it.) A catechumen is someone who has never been baptized; he or she may be an adult, a teenager or a young child. The journey to the waters of baptism normally takes place over the course of a year.

After an initial period of inquiry into the Catholic faith, those ready to do so publicly declare their intent to join the church and are accepted into the "order of catechumens." Then, with the help of catechists, sponsors and the entire community of believers, the catechumens begin to share in the life of the community and do what Christians do: read the scriptures, gather on Sundays with other believers and bear witness to the message of Jesus in word and deed. Often the catechumens are dismissed on Sundays after the homily to continue reflecting on the day's scriptures.

The liturgical year plays an intimate part in their introduction to the Christian way of life. Lent is a period of intensified preparation, beginning with a ritual when the catechumens are chosen ("elected") for initiation. Now they are called "the elect." At the Easter Vigil, the elect are baptized, confirmed and welcomed to the Lord's table for the first time. The Easter Vigil marks a high point in their journey — in much the same way that a wedding day is a high point in a couple's relationship — but, of course, the adventure has just begun.

Q&A: Candidates in Church

Who are the candidates we hear so much about in church?

Catechumens are people who have never been baptized and are now preparing to be baptized, confirmed and welcomed to the Lord's table at the Easter Vigil through the Rite of Christian Initiation of Adults (commonly called the RCIA). Often there are others who have already been baptized and who now desire to become fully initiated members of the Catholic church. They, too, undergo a period of formation based on the Rite of Christian Initiation of Adults; they are called *candidates* because they are discerning a call to complete their initiation.

Like those whom we welcome into our own families through marriage or adoption, the candidates bring with them a wide variety of experiences and traditions. Some of them may have been baptized in another faith tradition; they now wish to enter into full communion with the Catholic church. Normally they are confirmed and receive their first communion at the time of their reception. (In the past, these candidates were often referred to as "converts," but that term is not appropriate if they were previously baptized. Baptism is the sacrament of conversion. Suggesting that people baptized in other Christian traditions are not already "converted" to Christ is false and uncharitable.)

Other candidates may have been baptized Catholic, usually as infants, but received no further formation in the Catholic faith. They, too, are preparing for confirmation and first communion.

The length of the preparation period varies depending on the background and spiritual needs of the individual. Those who have taken an active role in their church in the past may need a relatively short period of preparation. Others may need a more extended period of formation and catechesis, similar to that of the catechumens. In both cases, active participation in the Sunday liturgy, prayerful reading of the scriptures and an increasing awareness of the church's teachings and mission are the primary means of preparation.

At the end of this period of preparation, those candidates who were baptized in another tradition are welcomed into the Catholic church through a simple act of reception. All the candidates are then confirmed and welcomed to the Lord's table for the first time. This celebration ideally takes place at the Easter Vigil, but may happen on any appropriate Sunday during the year.

The newly confirmed now take their place in the assembly and continue to do what Christians have done throughout the ages: offer thanks and praise to God and spread the good news of God's love and reconciliation.

Period of Evangelization

Where do you go when you have questions about God? About the meaning of life? About prayer or sin or Mary or the saints? How do you respond when you are touched by another person's faith or selflessness or goodness? Whom do you go to in times of sadness or uncertainty? What do you do when you feel blessed?

We Catholics have many answers to those questions. We may seek out our pastor or another parish minister, or turn to another believer, perhaps a friend or family member. Maybe we seek the intercession of the saints or go directly to God in prayer.

But where does someone go who doesn't belong to a community of faith? Many of them, too, seek out a Catholic minister or friend. This may be the first step in wanting to learn more about what Catholics believe and perhaps even the first step in joining the Catholic church. If so, they may be invited to join others who have similar questions. These people, called *inquirers,* meet with some members of the community, clergy and laity, to seek answers to their questions and learn about what the church believes.

This first, informal step in the Christian initiation process is called *precatechumenate* because it precedes the decision and commitment that people in the *catechumenate* are called to make. The precatechumenate period is a time of inquiry. It may last a short time or for a period of many months or years; it is up to the inquirer. It is also called the *period of evangelization* because in this time we tell the good news that we have to share: the Christian faith as it is lived in the Catholic communion. We tell it through the great stories of scripture, through the history and tradition of the church, through the lives of ordinary Christians. And because the questions that urged the inquirers to learn more about God and the church are signs of God already present and active in their lives, we listen, too, and help the inquirers see how God has always been with them and where God is leading them.

Copyright 1997 Archdiocese of Chicago: Liturgy Training Publications, 1800 North Hermitage Avenue, Chicago IL 60622-1101; 1-800-933-1800. Text by Victoria M. Tufano. Art by Annika Nelson.

Rite of Acceptance

Have you ever been intrigued by a travel brochure or the travel section of the Sunday newspaper? They lay before us all the marvels and wonders of distant and different lands. They may show us places and things that we've never seen; they hint at adventures that can't fully be described. Usually we spend a minute or an hour imagining what the journey might be like and then we turn the page or set the brochure down.

Those who come to us to find out about the Catholic church begin with a period of inquiry. The period of inquiry might be compared to reading a travel brochure. What kind of journey might this be? What might we encounter on the way? Where might we end up? These are important questions, but asking them is not the same thing as taking the journey.

The Rite of Acceptance into the Order of Catechumens — celebrated at the end of the period of inquiry — is something like sign-up day. At this liturgy, the inquirers who have asked the questions and now are ready to embark on the journey arrive at our door. We greet them and ask them what they want. They want what we told them that we could help them discover: faith, baptism, eternal life. We mark them with the cross, for this is the sign of all who are on this journey. We give them the holy scriptures: It is the guidebook that we use on the way. We promise to be with them on this trip, for we are still on it ourselves. And we give them wise guides — sponsors, catechists, pastors and many others — to surround them and support them as they learn the ways of the road.

Any good travel agent will tell you that she or he cannot guarantee how a journey will end, or what exactly will happen along the way. We can't say, either, what will happen along this way. But in faith we can say that if we and those we invite on this journey are faithful to the one who has called us to make it, then the end of the journey will be more marvelous than we imagined at the onset.

The Catechumenate

Have you ever tried to learn to do something from a book? How to knit a sweater or set up a computer can be learned from a book, but such things are better learned from someone who has mastered the skill. More important things, such as how to treat others kindly, how to stand up for our beliefs and how to be hopeful in difficult times, are almost always learned from the example of others.

How do we learn to live a life of faith? There are many books on the subject, but none of them can teach how to live the faith as well as the people who are trying to live it. When those who have been coming to the church to inquire about what we believe and how we live decide that they want to prepare to become Catholic, they enter the catechumenate. The word *catechumenate* is used for the process of becoming a Catholic Christian; it also means a specific period within that process.

During the period of the catechumenate, *catechumens* (unbaptized people) and *candidates* (baptized people) prepare to join the Catholic church by learning and doing what Catholics learn and do.

The strongest feature of this period is *catechesis*. This means that the catechumens and candidates learn to believe and celebrate the mysteries of the faith by listening as the scriptures are proclaimed and preached and by participating as the church celebrates what it believes throughout the liturgical year. They also learn the many other times and ways we pray. In addition, the church's moral teachings, traditions and disciplines are explained.

In many parishes, the primary time for catechesis is after the liturgy of the word on Sundays. As the rest of the assembly proceeds with the Mass, the catechumens and, usually, the candidates go to another room to prepare to take their place as full, participating members of the body of Christ.

The catechumens and candidates also learn the ways of Christians by getting to know us and seeing how we deal in faith with daily life. They participate in parish events. They also participate in our life of service to the church and to the world.

By spending time with us, the catechumens and candidates forge bonds of friendship, strengthening their ties with the church. By our spending time with them, our faith is strengthened and renewed. They remind us that our faith is a living, growing reality, and that people are attracted to it today just as they were centuries ago by the teachings of Jesus and the life of his disciples.

Copyright 1997 Archdiocese of Chicago: Liturgy Training Publications, 1800 North Hermitage Avenue, Chicago IL 60622-1101; 1-800-933-1800. Text by Victoria M. Tufano. Art by Annika Nelson.

Rite of Election

How strange this title sounds to us! While many of us would probably agree that our national, state and local elections are rituals of a special breed, we hardly expect to find a "rite of election" in church. But long before any of our ancestors thought of electing their leaders, God was electing a people, selecting Israel, a rag-tag clan in a tiny corner of the earth, to be special, holy, a chosen people. God did not choose them because they were noteworthy in any way; they were not powerful, strong or particularly clever. But once they were chosen, they were God's forever. Even when they strayed, looking to other gods for hope or help, God clung to them fiercely, calling them back again and again when anyone else would have gladly let them go.

It is the same with us. God chooses us, elects us, in Christ, to be a holy people, to be a church, to be signs of the reign of God on earth. The catechumens who have been preparing for baptism and those who have been working with them for months and years believe that God has chosen them to be one of us, the baptized. At the rite of election, their godparents, sponsors, catechists, pastors and friends will testify before the bishop that God has chosen these people. They will offer the evidence of their lives among us, hearing and following God's word, praying with God's people and taking part in the work and the communal life of God's church. After listening to this testimony, the bishop will declare that they are elected for baptism, chosen to be God's own in Christ Jesus — not because they earned it, but because God wants it. And that is election by a landslide!

Copyright © 1997 Archdiocese of Chicago: Liturgy Training Publications, 1800 North Hermitage Avenue, Chicago IL 60622-1101; 1-800-933-1800. Text by Victoria M. Tufano. Art by Annika Nelson.

Scrutinies

Every time we celebrate the sacrament of baptism, we ask the questions, "Do you renounce Satan? and all his works? and all his empty promises?" These are serious questions. We should consider them carefully before answering. And that is what the elect, those preparing to be baptized at the Easter Vigil, spend much of Lent doing.

For those who are making their final preparation for baptism, Lent is a time of purification and enlightenment. They examine their lives in the light of God's word and ask the entire Christian community to pray that whatever is weak and sinful within them may be eliminated and that whatever is good and holy may be affirmed. And we do. After the homily, in a litany of intercession, we proclaim the power of Jesus over all sin. Then we pray over the elect for their deliverance and strengthening. The presider, catechists, sponsors and other members of the community also may lay their hands on the heads of the elect in an ancient sign of forgiveness, healing and empowerment.

And because the entire community will renew its baptismal promises at Easter, we too examine our lives in light of God's word. Of course, this is something we should be doing throughout the year, but we focus on this self-examination in a special way during Lent. In every community that will baptize adults or older children at the Easter Vigil, special rites known as the "scrutinies" are celebrated at liturgy on the third, fourth and fifth Sundays of Lent.

On these Sundays, the gospel readings are from the Gospel of John; they are the stories of the Samaritan woman whom Jesus meets at Jacob's well, the healing and coming to faith of the man born blind and the raising of Lazarus from the dead. These readings have been used for centuries to prepare the elect and the church for baptism. The readings focus on sin and redemption using the images of thirst and water, darkness and light, death and life. By examining ourselves through these readings, we come to know how we have become parched, how we have been blinded, how we have become deadened through sin. When we and the elect are asked at Easter to renounce Satan, evil works and empty promises, our answer can be a thoughtful, strong and heartfelt "I do."

This Is the Night

This is the night. The fire has been kindled and the flame has been shared, gradually but confidently overcoming the darkness. The great stories of God's love for creation from before the very first moment have been told, and the great story of God's love poured out in salvation has been proclaimed and preached. This is the moment.

The elect come forward. Do you believe, they are asked, in the God who is Father, Son and Spirit? in the church, who continues the Son's work and worship of the Father through the Spirit? Do you wish to be joined to the faithful living who rely on God's forgiveness and the faithful dead who hope in their bodily resurrection? Do you seek eternal life?

Then come to these waters to be reborn. Enter this bath to be made clean. Step into this tomb and die to all that has been so that you may live for all that truly is.

Don the robe of the new creation that you have become. Accept the light to guide you on the Way.

Be sealed, signed, anointed and enlivened with the Spirit who now lives and acts in you. Be offered at the altar to the one you now call Father. Be embraced by the church, God's people, Christ's body, in the peace you have longed for. Be fed at the table of the one you now call Lord. For soon you will be sent out again, not to listen and learn this time but to proclaim and witness.

This is the night. This is the moment. Alleluia!

Mission and Mystagogy

"Go in peace to love and serve the Lord." With those words, all the baptized are dismissed from the eucharist. For those who were baptized at Easter, the significance of this is that it is a new dismissal. As catechumens, they were dismissed after the homily to continue being formed by the word of God and the teachings of the church. As *neophytes,* now they remain with the baptized and take their part in the work of the faithful: to offer intercession, praise, sacrifice and thanksgiving to the Father. In other words, the baptized continue the work of Jesus, in whose name they pray, who is present within and among them and in the sacrament at the altar.

But the work of the baptized and the goal of Christian initiation is not completed by participating in the liturgy of the eucharist. The eucharist itself is not complete until those who have celebrated it return to the world from which they came to continue to offer intercession, praise and thanksgiving through their attitudes, actions and interactions in everyday life. The mission of Jesus was to proclaim the Good News of God's reign and to bring all people

to the Father, and that is the mission into which we all are baptized.

During the Fifty Days of Easter, and for about a year, the neophytes participate in *mystagogy,* a Greek word that means "teaching the mysteries." The mysteries this refers to are primarily the sacraments. During this time, and throughout their lives, the neophytes and all the faithful deepen their understanding of what it means to have been baptized and confirmed and to continue to participate in all the sacraments, particularly the eucharist. At the end of every Mass, we are offered a small reminder that to participate in the sacraments is to take on the work and mission of Jesus.

Go in peace to love and serve the Lord. Thanks be to God.

Finding Our Place

Why do we fill up the seats in church from the back to the front? Maybe it's piety: We sit in the back because, aware of our many failings, we don't feel worthy to draw near. Maybe it's culture: We sit in the back because our mothers taught us never to claim the best seats or make ourselves the center of attention. Maybe it's selfish: We want to be able to skip out early. Whatever the reason, it causes a practical problem: The front seats are always empty, creating a gulf between the Lord's table and the Lord's people. And latecomers stand in the back rather than march up to the front where everyone can see that they're late.

Let's show some hospitality here! Let's fill the church up from the front to the back, leaving the back rows for those who come later or late. And let's fill each row from the center: If you're the first one in a row, don't hug the end (unless you're a minister and will need to get in and out). Move into the middle so that others may come and sit beside you.

Filling in the front seats first isn't proud or arrogant. It's part of the ministry of hospitality that all of us who are baptized are called to exercise. It's a simple act of kindness that helps the church to gather better around its Lord, so that we may give God thanks and praise.

We Bow Before You

How do we show reverence and love for Christ when we enter and leave the church? First, we greet each other as we would greet Christ. ("Where two or three of you gather, there I am.") Then, we bow to the altar.

Why? On this altar we place our bread and wine that becomes Christ's body and blood: This is the place of sacrifice. At this altar we sit with God to dine in eternity: This is Easter's banquet table.

The altar of the Most High is this table in our midst — the table of every grace and blessing! And more. The Rite of Dedication of an Altar (#4) says, "Because it is at the altar that the memorial of the Lord is celebrated and his body and blood given to the people, the church's writers see in the altar a sign of Christ himself — hence they affirm: 'The altar is Christ.'"

Christ is the Anointed One, baptized, anointed with the Holy Spirit and robed in light. We are Christians, anointed ones, baptized, anointed with chrism and robed in white. Just like Christ, just like us, our altar was washed, anointed and robed. On its dedication day, it was sprinkled with holy water. The bishop rubbed holy chrism into its top, and ministers robed it in a white cloth.

So let's bow to Christ at the altar before taking our places. And let's bow again when we depart. Christ the offering. Christ the meal. Christ the altar of sacrifice. Christ the paschal banquet table. Holy Christ, we bow before you!

Renewing Baptism

Whenever a group of people gather for a public event, it is usual for them to identify themselves in some way. Uniforms, team jackets or color-coded name tags announce to friend and stranger alike common interests or origins. At Sunday eucharist we remind ourselves of our kinship with one another and with Christ through baptism in the rite of blessing and sprinkling of holy water. This rite, familiar to some as the *asperges* from the pre–Vatican II liturgy (from the text that was chanted), calls to mind our union with the death and resurrection of Jesus. The revised ritual reminds us that the sprinkling rite is appropriate at any Sunday liturgy, for it expresses the paschal character of Sunday. It is particularly appropriate during the Easter season and on feasts in which baptismal images are highlighted.

After the sign of the cross and the greeting, the blessing and sprinkling with holy water is actually the first option, and the penitential rite is the second. The rite of sprinkling is simple: The presider invites the assembly to pray silently, then blesses the water. In some places, salt, a symbol of strength and flavor and effectiveness, among other things, is added. Then the assembly is blessed with the water. The priest and other ministers may walk through the assembly generously sprinkling the people, or people may come forward in a procession and sign themselves with the water. In either case, an abundant use of water signifies God's overflowing love and mercy. As in the sacrament of baptism itself, many levels of meaning come into play: Water signifies cleansing, protection from evil, newness of life, forgiveness of sin and God's saving deeds.

After the sprinkling rite and opening prayer, the liturgy of the word begins. Immediately we do what baptized people are called to do. We listen to God's word, offer prayers for the needs of all, give thanks and praise and share in the body and blood of our Lord. Conscious of our shared baptismal heritage, we are sent forth to announce the good news which we ourselves have seen and heard.

Q&A: What to Read

1-2010

How are the readings for each Sunday chosen?

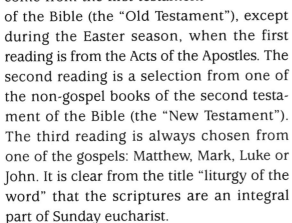

Each Sunday the word of God is proclaimed in our church in the form of three scripture readings and a psalm. The first reading and the psalm always come from the first testament of the Bible (the "Old Testament"), except during the Easter season, when the first reading is from the Acts of the Apostles. The second reading is a selection from one of the non-gospel books of the second testament of the Bible (the "New Testament"). The third reading is always chosen from one of the gospels: Matthew, Mark, Luke or John. It is clear from the title "liturgy of the word" that the scriptures are an integral part of Sunday eucharist.

This emphasis on a more thorough and varied use of the scriptures is a direct result of the renewal of the liturgy called for by the Second Vatican Council: "The treasures of the Bible are to be opened up more lavishly, so that richer fare may be provided for the faithful at the table of God's word." To meet this need, a new lectionary (or book of readings for worship) was published in 1970. It included assigned texts for each Sunday based on a three-year cycle of readings. And, as noted above, each Sunday included three readings as well as a responsorial psalm.

This was a major change. Previously, only one set of Sunday readings was used year after year. Two readings and a psalm verse were appointed for each Sunday. And one of those readings, the gospel, was almost always from the Gospel of Matthew.

The gospel readings in the 1970 lectionary include selections from all four evangelists: Matthew in what is called Year A, Mark in Year B and Luke in Year C. We hear the Gospel of John during the major liturgical seasons as well as during Year B (the year of Mark), perhaps because Mark's gospel is the shortest of the four and wouldn't otherwise fill out the whole year.

The gospels were assigned first. The first reading was chosen for its connection to the day's gospel. The psalm that follows the first reading is related to it. The psalm is the assembly's response to the word that has just been proclaimed. The second reading is not necessarily related to the other readings. Selections from the chosen book are simply read somewhat in order.

As people baptized to live not by bread alone but by the word of God as well, the liturgy of the word should not be the only time we hear the readings. One way to live with the lectionary is to do an attentive reading of the scriptures before the liturgy each Sunday — a fruitful and enriching way of entering more deeply into the prayer. Another approach is to hear the word proclaimed in the assembly first, and then spend the following week rereading and meditating on it. Whichever method you choose, several helpful resources have been published to aid you.

Silence

"Be quiet, you're in church now!" Many of us grew up being reminded regularly that the appropriate behavior for us during Mass was to be silent. Church and the library had that in common. Then, with the reforms of the Second Vatican Council, active participation became the norm. Usually active participation is understood as joining in the singing and saying the responses along with everyone else. Rarely do we expand the definition of participation to include communal silence.

Public silence is frequently very awkward. We assume someone forgot their cue or made an embarrassing mistake. Yet we also know the heart-gripping impact when a grandstand full of people observes a moment of silence. The liturgy invites us to pray without words several times during Sunday Mass. Before the opening prayer, after the readings and the homily, perhaps during the intercessions and again after communion, we are given the opportunity to call to mind God's presence in our midst, to offer our personal petitions and express our thanks for God's continuing blessings. Such silence is not a passive "shutting down" but rather an attentive awareness of our intimate connection with the Lord and with one another. Such awareness requires ample time to develop — ample time not only at a particular liturgy, but Sunday after Sunday after Sunday. Only then will the inevitable coughing, kneeler banging and fussing babies mark the beginning of our silence and not the end of it!

In another, more profound sense, we are always silent at liturgy — even when we speak. We sing psalms and speak prayers that are not our own but rather the words of our ancestors in faith and the words of the church. Our individualistic American culture finds such behavior suspicious or even threatening: "I am my own person!" But it is precisely in that surrender to the power of ritual and the life of the larger community that we discover our true voice.

Sing Psalms

Until relatively recently, Catholics were notorious for their unfamiliarity with the Bible. One of the goals of the Second Vatican Council was to open up the rich treasure of the scriptures, which had so long been relegated to a kind of second place. The proclamation of three scripture readings at each Sunday liturgy has exposed us to more and varied selections from the Bible. Less obvious but perhaps equally significant was the re-introduction of the assembly's participation in the psalm after the first reading at Sunday eucharist.

The book of Psalms has been called the Bible's hymnal. In it are ancient songs that express great joy and great sorrow, as well as almost every emotion in between. We know that Jesus and his disciples prayed using the psalms. The original melodies of these songs have long been lost to us, but because of the great power of the psalms to express the struggles and joys of the human condition, they continue to be an important part of both Jewish and Christian worship.

At the Sunday liturgy, the psalm flows naturally out of the period of silence which follows the first reading. The psalm is directly related to the day's readings or to the liturgical season; its images and emotions give us a clearer sense that God's saving deeds continue to be revealed in our own lives. The psalm is called "responsorial" not because it is a response to the reading (although it is that), but because it is structured so that a cantor sings the verses and the assembly sings the response. The repeated refrain is meant to take root in our memories and in our hearts.

"The Lord is my shepherd, there is nothing I shall want." "If today you hear God's voice, harden not your hearts." "Be with me, Lord, when I am in trouble." Already the words of the more frequently used psalms are beginning to find a home in us. You are encouraged to take the words of this Sunday's psalm response (write them on the cover of your bulletin if you must) and weave them into the pattern of your days during the coming week. Allow this sung prayer, which is rooted in the lives of our ancestors in faith, to echo in your days and deeds.

Q&A: Inclusive Language

Can you explain the use of "inclusive language" in church?

The fact that biblical Greek, Old Slavonic and Latin are no longer spoken but have evolved and developed into modern Greek, Russian (and other Slavic languages) and Italian (and other Romance languages), is evidence that, like people, languages evolve.

In our own time, languages and vocabulary continue to develop and change. English speakers rarely use "thee" or "thou" any more, or use "suffer" in the sense of "allow." The vocabulary found in Shakespeare's work is not the vocabulary used in our daily newspapers.

One contemporary linguistic development is based on the fact that English, unlike biblical Greek, Latin or Polish, does not have an easy-to-use generic term for "human being." People have questioned whether it is appropriate to continue to say "men" when "men and women" is actually meant. Using masculine words at times to refer solely to males, while at other times intending them to include females, can be confusing. It is also considered discriminatory by many people.

The church has a duty to be sensitive to the culture in which it proclaims its message. Many of us are concerned that the

English translations of scripture and of liturgy might be heard as discriminatory or exclusive, even though the original texts do not carry such meanings. As a result, translations are being revised to make explicit what the original texts seem to have intended in references to groups of people. Usually this is done by using words such as "brothers and sisters," "men and women," "sons and daughters." This is called *horizontal inclusive language,* because it is the language that we use when we human beings refer to other human beings.

The use of inclusive language can also apply to words used to refer to God. (This is called *vertical inclusive language.*) Although Jesus addressed God as "Father" to indicate the intimacy he felt with God, Christian theologians have always held that any such human title can only feebly capture the reality of the divine. Since God is beyond our human categories of male and female, language can misrepresent the divine reality if it is commonly interpreted as meaning that the First Person of the Trinity is male. It is a struggle to use the English language well and in a manner that expresses the Christian belief in a personal God without overusing masculine pronouns or nouns. Some attempts at rephrasing prayers or scripture passages have produced less than stunning results, but with experience and insight, our efforts toward renewing our English-language religious expressions should improve in the future.

17

Dismissal of Catechumens

Perhaps the change in our liturgical life since Vatican II that seems the strangest is the Sunday dismissal of those preparing for initiation into the Catholic church. Each week during much of the year, after the scripture readings and homily, the presider invites those who have publicly expressed a desire for full membership in the church to leave the assembled community and to continue to reflect on the riches of God's word with a trained leader called a catechist.

Those of us who are old enough might remember the pre–Vatican II division of the Mass into (1) The Mass of the Catechumens and (2) The Mass of the Faithful. This terminology reflected the ancient practice of dismissing the catechumens (who are preparing for baptism, confirmation and eucharist at the Easter Vigil) immediately after the homily. What at first seems like an inhospitable act — sending someone out of our midst — is, on another level, an act of true hospitality. Those who are not yet able to eat with us at the Lord's table are sent out to be further nourished with the word of God. (It might be more inhospitable to eat and drink in front of them!)

The presence of those preparing for initiation is a blessing for any parish community. Each Sunday they remind us of the church's (often unspoken) invitation to visitors to join our ranks. But perhaps even more profound than that, the question, "Why are they leaving?" leads to the thought, "Why am I staying?" Seen through the eyes of the catechumens, who are not yet able to be nourished at the Lord's table, our Sunday obligation is transformed into a Sunday privilege.

The Collection

It is a familiar routine. A collection is taken up — for a baby gift, a departing colleague or a local event. With varying degrees of willingness, we put our money in the basket and feel that we have done our duty.

That same invitation is made to us in an entirely different context every Sunday as we gather to offer God thanks and praise. During the liturgy of the word, we listen to the voice of God in the scriptures, proclaim our belief in the creed and offer prayers for the needs of the church and the world. Then a collection is taken up.

It is commonly understood that the money given during the collection will be used to support the ongoing work of the church. This includes setting aside a portion of those funds to be used directly for those in need. But in this age of credit cards and automatic fund transfers, isn't there a more efficient way to do this?

If it were only a matter of paying the bills, yes, there are probably simpler ways to collect money. But our monetary contributions are more than just financial transactions; they symbolize our willingness to place our lives at God's disposal and to be ourselves transformed into the body and blood of Christ. The act of bringing our hard-earned money (in cash or check, in an envelope or not) and placing it in the basket together is a ritual sign of the real offering that will happen when the priest invites us, "Lift up your hearts," and we respond, "We have lifted them up to the Lord."

Clearly, such a vision is beyond the realm of simple accounting. The pooling of our resources is a preparation for the pooling of our lives in loving service to one another and to the poor.

Always Thanksgiving

The liturgy of the eucharist refers to the part of the Mass that begins with the collection and the preparation of the altar and the gifts of bread and wine. What are we doing in these actions? Much of the answer lies in the word *eucharist*. Derived from a Greek word, it means "thanksgiving."

The eucharistic prayer, beginning with "The Lord be with you. And also with you. Lift up your hearts . . . ," and ending with the Great Amen, is the central part of the Mass. It is proclaimed over bread and wine, the basic signs of life and death, food and drink from the tables of ordinary people. We praise God for creation. We give God thanks and praise for Jesus, and for Jesus' saving deeds. We ask God that the abundance promised at this holy table may be shared with the whole world, with all who seek God, even with the dead.

The eucharistic prayer — although said aloud only by the priest — is not "the priest's prayer." The entire prayer requires every baptized person's full, conscious and active participation. That does not mean that everyone reads the words aloud — that wouldn't work! Rather, it means that we must join our hearts to the words sung or spoken by the priest, that we must assume an attentive posture, put aside the missalette and sing our parts with gusto and sincerity.

In the end, eucharist is what our life as Christians is all about. In suffering or in joy, in confusion or routine, our life is always to be praise, always to be thanksgiving, always to be a sharing of God's abundance with those in need.

Communion from the Cup

Jesus' command to us at the Last Supper is clear: "Take this, all of you, and drink from it." In the three decades since the Second Vatican Council, communion from a common cup for all the faithful was gradually re-introduced as a sign of obedience to the Lord's command. But centuries before that, sharing both the body and the blood was so much the norm that to refuse the cup raised suspicions about one's beliefs.

For a number of reasons, the practice of sharing the cup became the exception rather than the rule. Popular piety placed an increased emphasis on seeing the sacred elements. Because of the difficulty of seeing the wine in the chalice, the wine became secondary. A change in the posture for communion from standing to kneeling made reception from the cup more awkward. Fears of spillage and disease also played a role. Complicated theological disputes eventually resulted in a decision at the Council of Trent in 1562 to avoid further misunderstandings and to withhold the cup from the laity.

Good liturgy demands that our actions be consistent with our words. At the preparation of the gifts, we bring forward the gifts of bread and wine. We pray that "the fruit of the vine and work of human hands" become "our spiritual food and drink." These gifts are offered to the Father, who changes them into the body and blood of the Lord and gives them back to us. The fullness of the mystery is lost when we do not accept the gifts in return. Good liturgy also demands respect for the power of our symbols. Wine calls to mind not only the joys of the heavenly banquet table, but also the price of the covenant which led to Jesus' suffering and death. We neglect the power of such images when we ignore the cup.

Prudence, of course, dictates that education and common sense be used so that sharing in the one cup is not a cause of fear or discomfort. The Centers for Disease Control in Atlanta have not found it necessary to recommend that the church abandon its ancient practice; however, out of courtesy, a communicant with a contagious illness, whether a mild cold or something more serious, may wish to refrain from drinking from the cup.

"When we eat this bread and drink this cup, we proclaim your death, Lord Jesus, until you come in glory." May our actions be consistent with the words we sing. May we eat and drink in obedience to the Lord's command.

Communion Song

The simple human activities of sharing in one loaf and one cup at Sunday eucharist clearly express our relationship with each other and with the Lord: We are one bread, one body. Our unity is evidenced not only in the one loaf and the one cup. We share a common posture of standing throughout the communion rite. Each of us is addressed with the same words, "The body of Christ. The blood of Christ." And we join our voices in psalms and hymns of praise.

The power of song to unite a group of people is well known. School songs, national anthems and old favorites sung around a campfire all serve to confirm common identity and strengthen the bond among those who are present. Our communion song, too, expresses outwardly our inward union with each other and the Lord. Because communion is a time of procession to the table of the Lord, communion songs are by definition processional songs. And

processions need music — music that moves our feet and our hearts.

Some might protest that they can't walk and chew gum at the same time, so how can they be expected to walk in procession, hold a book and sing. Ideally, at the time of communion, the assembly joins in with a simple repeated refrain that does not require a worship aid, freeing our hands and our eyes from the printed page. Others complain that singing during communion distracts them from prayer. The moment of communion is, of course, an intensely personal time but in Catholic liturgy, it is not a private time. Allowing for a generous time of silence after communion can meet this need for silent prayer. Liturgy as the public prayer of the church demands of us a disciplined surrender of our individual lives to our common life in Christ. Just as those who distribute the bread and the cup minister to us, we minister to each other when we join in singing the communion song. Thus we taste and see and *hear* the goodness of the Lord.

22

Q&A: More Than Once

May I receive communion more than once a day?

A key insight that the church has recovered since Vatican II is that participation in the Mass reaches a high point in the sharing of communion, an action that Christians should consider normal and commonplace rather than secondary and rare.

This vital connection between one's presence at Mass and the reception of communion is expressed in several ways, including the understanding of Mass as a sacrificial meal in which we are fed with the Lord's body and blood, the dismissal of cate-chumens before the liturgy of the eucharist

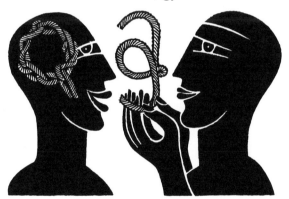

(they are dismissed precisely because they cannot receive communion until they are baptized), the procession with the gifts and the distribution of bread consecrated at the Mass rather than bread that has been reserved in the tabernacle.

As the interconnections between the reception of communion and participation in the Mass became clearer, people began to wonder why individuals should be prevented from receiving communion at a Mass simply because they might have received communion earlier that same day. In the early 1970s, Rome changed a long-standing practice and explicitly permitted those who were present at a special Mass, such as Masses in which sacraments were conferred or similar special occasions, to receive communion, even if they had already communicated earlier that day.

This revised practice has been included in a more general form in the 1983 Code of Canon Law. There is no longer any mention of the second Mass being in any way related to a special occasion (canon 917). Thus, current church custom permits anyone to receive communion a second time on any day, as long as the second reception of communion occurs during Mass. (Thus, this permission does not hold if communion is being distributed outside of Mass except in the case of viaticum.)

The scriptures record that, at the Last Supper, Jesus said, "All of you, take and eat . . . take and drink." On those occasions when a person attends a second Mass on the same day (either by obligation or by devotion), he or she should never hesitate about fully participating in the celebration of the eucharist by receiving communion a second time.

23

Q&A: Stipends

What is the contemporary understanding of "Mass stipends"?

Stipend is the older term associated with the monetary offering given to a priest with the stipulation that a Mass would be offered for a specified intention. The current Code of Canon Law continues to permit the practice but has modified the terminology, referring to an "offering" rather than a "stipend."

The practice has its origins in the custom of the faithful providing the necessities of bread, water and wine for the eucharist, as well as food for the clergy and the needy of the community. It is also significant that daily Mass was not a universal practice until recent centuries. As a result, Masses in which prayers were offered for specific intentions, for example, for a good harvest, in time of disease or as part of funeral rites, would need to be specially requested of the community's clergy and they would be compensated appropriately.

Mass offerings are not required by current church law, although the practice is widespread. Any Mass is of infinite worth, and through the revised general intercessions, the assembly prays for many intentions at each Mass. Yet there are times that our prayers and thoughts are focused on one intention, particularly at weddings and funerals, or on the anniversary of a death. Thus, it makes sense to speak of an intention associated with a celebration of the Mass. It is also a common practice to publish the intentions for scheduled Masses in parish bulletins.

The Mass offering is a free-will donation and should never be seen as "paying for" a Mass. In fact, priests are not allowed to accept more than one offering for any Mass, nor are they permitted to receive more than one offering per day even though they may be obligated to say more than one Mass.

To encourage uniformity, some dioceses have established a suggested standard offering. Those who wish to request prayers for a specific intention and donate an offering should check with their priest about the customs and policies in their diocese and parish.

24

Advent

A Sense of the Season

December is the time for expressing the hope and strengthening the dreams that will carry us through the next year. Advent is the way we as church express our hopes. Prophetic visions, prayers and songs calling for the Lord to come do help us to hope profoundly. Advent allows us to do what most others do in December — but to see in the coming Lord the answer to our dreams. In our Catholic tradition, keeping Advent means singing the songs of expectation, of our hopes and longing, before we enter into the full-throated praise of Christmas carols.

Here are a few lines from our tradition on what Advent is about. "Advent has a twofold character: as a season to prepare us for Christmas when Christ's first coming is remembered; as a season when that remembrance directs the mind and the heart to await Christ's second coming at the end of time. Advent is thus a period for devout and joyful expectation." (*General Norms for the Liturgical Year and the Calendar,* #39)

Thomas Merton, in his book *Seasons of Celebration,* reviewed the ways Saint Bernard of Clairvaux approached these comings of Christ. The first advent was Christ's birth. The other will be at the end of time. Faith in these two stimulates recognition of a third, the advent of Christ in our church now, today. Viewed from this perspective, the Advent liturgy, with its scriptures, prayers and songs, is neither a romantic return to the Old Testament while we wait for the baby at Bethlehem, nor is it an exercise in expressing hope for an ever-receding end of time. The Advent liturgy is neither nostalgic nor illusory. When we take the tradition and enter it fully, we become Advent, the people in and through whom Christ comes.

Copyright © 1997 Archdiocese of Chicago, Liturgy Training Publications, 1800 North Hermitage Avenue, Chicago IL 60622-1101; 1-800-933-1800. Text by G. Thomas Ryan. Art by Chuck Ludeke.

25

Eternity's Clock and Crown

What is this Advent wreath whose four candles help us mark the passing of the weeks before Christmas? It is eternity's clock — a circle that says "In our ending is our beginning." It is the wheel of time — a circle of evergreen branches — cut and left to wither — revealing that death and life are both of a piece. It is also a crown, the victor's laurel garland, the sign that the race is done, the prize won. It is the crown of us as a people, a chosen race, a royal priesthood.

It is the crown of each of us as individuals — baptized individuals (all of a piece) whose heads were smeared with that royal oil, chrism. We are marked for eternity. With four candles lit, the Advent wreath is the fiery crown that we give to Christ the King, the Savior who returns in the growing gloom to gather us into our eternal home, the new and heavenly Jerusalem.

26

Christmas

A Sense of the Season

You probably know the song "The Twelve Days of Christmas." Even though a radio station once proclaimed the twelve days of Christmas as those before December 25, Christians have always kept Christmas as a season from December 25 until January 6 (the traditional Epiphany). The church calendar today even extends the celebration until the feast of the Baptism of the Lord — the Sunday after Epiphany.

Here is what the church says about the season of Christmas: "Next to the yearly celebration of the paschal mystery [meaning the Triduum and Easter season], the church holds most sacred the memorial of Christ's birth and early manifestations. This is the purpose of the Christmas season." (*General Norms for the Liturgical Year and the Calendar*, #32)

More than just "Jesus' birthday," the Christmas season is a time for remembering and reveling in the nativity of Christ, the revelation of Christ to the Jewish shepherds, the revelation of Christ to the Gentile magi (that's us!), Christ's baptism by John in the Jordan, and Christ changing water into wine at the wedding "on the third day" (John 2:1) in Cana of Galilee. In all these saving events, we know that "the Word is made flesh and dwells among us."

How can we keep Christmas not just as a day, but as a season? Keep the tree up (and watered!) and shining bright until the Baptism of the Lord. Sing carols and read the scriptures every day. Safely put candles around your creche: Use small glass votive candle holders, and place them away from the straw. You might also want to add a little water to the bottom of the glass before putting the candle in — an added precaution that will also help you clean the glass more easily. When you light the candles, sing or say the prayer of the angels: Glory in heaven and peace on earth, now and forever. Amen!

27

The Paradise Tree

What is the decorated evergreen tree — the light and sight and smell of which means "Christmas"? It is the tree in the center of the garden, lost to us by our first parents' folly, restored to us by Christ's saving deed. It is the tree that claps its hands uproariously before the Lord, who comes. It is the tree — once drafted into death's service — that now blooms forth and shines in splendor: He who died in its arms has defeated death and lives forever. This is the tree of life straddling the river of life in the new Jerusalem. Bearing twelve kinds of fruit, it is laden with enough joy for all the tribes. It marks the spot where heaven intersects with earth. And look! That spot is here — in the house of the church. That spot is here — in your own house. Today is born our Savior, Christ the Lord! Paradise is so very close to home.

28

Ordinary Time: Winter

A Sense of the Season

What do the words *Ordinary Time* mean? Dorothy Day said, "The words 'Ordinary Time' in our prayer books put me in a state of confusion and irritation. To me, no time is ordinary." She was right. The *Ordinary* in Ordinary Time refers to ordinal — counted — time, not to a lack of something to celebrate. The Roman document, *General Norms for the Liturgical Year and Calendar,* says: "Apart from those seasons having their own distinctive character [Advent, Christmastime, Lent, Triduum and Eastertime], 33 or 34 weeks remain in the yearly cycle that do not celebrate a specific aspect of the mystery of Christ. Rather, especially on the Sundays, they are devoted to the mystery of Christ in all its aspects." (#43)

How do we celebrate "the mystery of Christ in all its aspects"? We gather every Sunday. Sunday is our original feast day. Christians have gathered every Sunday — the day of Christ's resurrection, the first day of the week — ever since there were Christians.

Each year there are two blocks of Ordinary Time, one in the winter between Christmastime and Lent, and the other in summer and fall, from Pentecost through Christ the King. When we gather on Sundays in Ordinary Time, as always, we hear the scriptures proclaimed. We systematically read through the gospels. The first readings from the first testament of the Bible were chosen for their relationship to the gospel passages. The second readings come from the various letters of the second testament of the Bible. The mystery of Christ "in all its aspects" unfolds.

What is the heart of our Sunday celebration? We do our eucharist; that is, we do our thanksgiving. We praise and thank God for all creation; we pray for the whole world, as we remember Christ's life, death and resurrection. We share the bread and wine, the body and blood. We are sent forth to be the body and blood of Christ in our homes, our workplaces, our neighborhoods, our towns, our cities, our country, our world.

"What happens in our churches every Sunday is the fruit of our week. What happens as the fruit of the week past is the beginning of the week to come. Sunday is simultaneously a point of arrival and departure for Christians on their way to the fullness of the kingdom. This is not ordinary at all. This is the fabric of Christian living." (*Saint Andrew Bible Missal* [Brooklyn: William J. Hirten Co., 1982.])

29

The Gospel of Matthew

The first gospel starts with "a genealogy of Jesus Christ, son of David, son of Abraham." With this opening the evangelist prepares us for this Jesus who will be the fulfillment of major figures of the Hebrew scriptures.

Archeologists and textual experts usually date the writing of the Gospel of Matthew to around 80 CE. One piece of evidence for the dating of this gospel is that it contains nearly all of the Gospel of Mark. From this we know that it was composed after 70 CE (near the time when Mark was written). In addition to having Mark as a source, the Gospel of Matthew shares a large chunk of material with Luke, material that appears neither in Mark or in John. From this we assume that there was another source for Matthew, one that he and the writer of Luke used. Matthew also had his own information about Jesus that the other evangelists did not.

The Gospel of Matthew is unique in its five-part structure: after the introduction (which contains the stories of the annunciation to Joseph [not Mary, as in Luke] of Jesus' birth, his birth and manifestation to the magi [not shepherds, as in Luke]), each part contains a long speech by Jesus followed by actions that Jesus performs. Part one is the Sermon on the Mount (chapters 5 – 7); part two prepares the disciples for their missionary journeys (10); part three is filled with parables (13); part four deals with church order (18); and the fifth part concerns the end of the world (24 – 25). Scholars assume that the evangelist adopted this structure from the Pentateuch, the first five books of the Bible. This is a big clue about the portrait of Jesus in this gospel.

Many of the people in the church for which the Gospel of Matthew was written were Jews. One of the main purposes of this gospel was to provide consolation to those who wrestled with the compatibility of the Jewish heritage and their faith in Jesus. For this reason we find references to patriarchs of ancient Israel from the very first verse. A genealogy filled with Jewish ancestors begins the text, and the evangelist fills the narrative with quotations from the Hebrew scriptures. All of this seeks to reassure the hearers that Jesus of Nazareth was indeed the Messiah anticipated in the older faith.

The Gospel of Matthew is proclaimed throughout Year A, in the years 1999, 2002, 2005, 2008 and so on.

In art, the evangelist Matthew is portrayed with an angel by his side. The feast of Saint Matthew is September 21.

30

The Gospel of Mark

The second gospel takes our breath away with its rapid telling of the events of Jesus' public ministry. A mere sixteen chapters from beginning to end, the Gospel of Mark is both the shortest and earliest of the four gospels in the Bible.

Archeologists and textual experts have dated this gospel to about 70 CE, at least a few decades after the death of Jesus. This date, which many Christians find to be quite late, does not mean that the stories were brand-new at the time; it means that earlier Christians so expected the second coming of Christ in their own lifetimes that they did not take the time to sit down and write. The stories were passed along orally until later in the first century.

The Gospel of Mark gives us a unique portrait of Jesus, which can be drawn as much from what the gospel does not contain as from what it does. The story begins, for example, not with a story of the birth of Jesus, as do the Gospels of Matthew

and Luke. No magi or shepherds for Mark! The end of the Gospel had a unique abbreviation as well. The original version of Mark ended not with 16:20 (as do our Bibles, centuries later), but with verse 16:8. The original text left hearers pondering disciples who had run away and tomb-visiting women who had fled the scene "frightened out of their wits." Verses 16:9 – 20 were added a short time later.

Between its abrupt beginning and incomplete ending — an empty tomb, but no resurrection — the gospel plunges us into the whirlwind of Jesus' activity, which is described in a sometimes harsh, spare style. Along the way Jesus preaches and prophesies, hollers and heals, teaches and tells tales up to his coming to Jerusalem, where his life as one of us ends, but the story just begins. (Perhaps we are the disciples who must now live in the mystery of the empty tomb.)

The portrait of Jesus sketched by Mark is difficult for Christians to hear. Because of its content of suffering and tribulation, some have called it a "passion narrative with a long introduction." Throughout the story, Jesus anticipates his death, and he draws the listener in to focus on this aspect of the Christian life.

The Gospel of Mark is proclaimed on Sundays in Year B, the years 2000, 2003, 2006, 2009 and so on.

In art, the evangelist Mark is portrayed with a lion by his side. The feast of Saint Mark is April 25.

Copyright © 1997 Archdiocese of Chicago: Liturgy Training Publications, 1800 North Hermitage Avenue, Chicago IL 60622-1101; 1-800-933-1800. Text by Martin Connell. Art by Rita Corbin.

31

The Gospel of Luke

If asked to name their favorite story from the Bible, most Christians would probably choose something from the Gospel of Luke. These stories are indeed unforgettable, and the Christian tradition is graced by this gospel from Luke's hand. It is the only one of the four gospels to describe the angel's annunciation of the coming birth of Jesus to Mary, and the visit of the shepherds at his birth; it is the only one to tell the parables of the Good Samaritan, of the prodigal son, and of the rich man and Lazarus; it is the only gospel to relate the story of Jesus and the disciples on the road to Emmaus after the resurrection. In addition to that, Luke's Christmas story is proclaimed by Linus on the Charlie Brown Christmas special!

Archeologists and textual experts usually date the writing of the Gospel of Luke to around 80 CE. One piece of evidence that helps with the dating is that the gospel contains nearly all of Mark, and from this we know that it was composed after 70 CE (about when Mark was written). In addition to having Mark as a source, the Gospel of Luke shares a large chunk of material with Matthew, material that appears neither in Mark nor in John. From this we assume that there was another source for Luke, one that he and the writer of Matthew used together. Luke also had a source of information that only he used.

The evangelist Luke is also the author of the Acts of the Apostles, which is, in a sense, the second part to the gospel. This is evident from the very polished Greek of these two books, but more specifically, from the fact that both books are addressed to Theophilus, a fellow believer. (See Luke 1:3 and Acts 1:1.) Luke's contribution, therefore, makes up more than one-quarter of the second testament.

The portrait of Jesus in the Gospel of Luke is of an itinerant prophet who is attracted to the poor and the outcast. He explains that his ministry is to them, and he envisions the heavenly banquet as filled with the poor and disenfranchised. The evangelist draws powerful portraits of despised members of the society, and much of the wonder of this compelling gospel is in its address to sinners.

The Gospel of Luke is proclaimed in Year C, the years 1998, 2001, 2004, 2007 and so on.

In art, the evangelist Luke is portrayed with a bull by his side. The feast of Saint Luke is October 18.

32

The Gospel of John

The Gospels of Matthew, Mark and Luke are called the *synoptic* gospels, coming from the two Greek words "optic," meaning "to see," and "syn," meaning "together" or "similarly." They are called so because the three describe basically the same events in Jesus' life; they are called so also to distinguish them from the other gospel: the Gospel of John.

The Gospel of John was probably the last of the four gospels to be written, and experts usually place its composition in the late first century. It is commonly held that the prologue (1:1–18) and the appendix (21:1–25) were added to the original gospel. This is particularly obvious about the appendix, for there is a clear conclusion to the Gospel of John at the end of chapter 20.

The portrait of Jesus in this gospel is unique for its supreme theology: Jesus is the Word of God, existing with God from the beginning of time (1:1–2). He is all-knowing and all-powerful; even the guards and soldiers who come to arrest Jesus fall down and worship him before they take him away (18:6). Most of the stories in John are not found in the other gospels; among the unique stories are the wedding feast at Cana, the Samaritan woman at the well, the raising of Lazarus and Jesus' washing of the feet of the disciples. Jesus has a lot to say in John; there are long discourses with familiar phrases such as "I am the good shepherd," "I am the resurrection," and "I am the true vine": weighty statements of a lofty theology.

While the Gospels of Matthew, Mark and Luke each have one year of the three-year lectionary cycle assigned for their proclamation, the Gospel of John does not. Rather, John is proclaimed on Sundays during the forty days of Lent and during the fifty days of the Easter season, as well as during the celebrations of particular feasts — such

as Holy Thursday, Good Friday, Pentecost and Christmas Day.

In art, the evangelist John is usually the only one of the four to be beardless, and there is an eagle by his side or near his head. Though they were probably two different people historically, tradition has merged the figures of the apostle John and the evangelist John. The feast of Saint John is December 27.

33

Lent

A Sense of the Season

The word *Lent* means springtime. This word comes from the same root as *lengthen.* Daytime lengthens during Lent. The northern hemisphere turns toward the sun, the source of life, and winter turns into spring. In Hebrew, the word for *repentance* is the same as the word that means *to turn,* like the turning of the earth to the sun, like the turning of the soil before planting.

"Even now, says the Lord, turn to me." (Joel 2:12) The word *sin* means separation. We are called to turn from our separate selves, from our sin, to come together in community. Self-denial is the way we express our repentance. In the lengthening brightness from Ash Wednesday until Holy Thursday afternoon, our holy Lent, we turn to God as our source of life.

Self-denial is threefold, advises Matthew's gospel. We pray: "Go to your room, close your door, and pray to your Father in private." We fast: "No one must see you are fasting but your Father." We give alms: "Keep your deeds of mercy secret, and your Father who sees in secret will repay you." Through the Lenten exercise of prayer, fasting and almsgiving, we spring-clean our lives, sharpen our senses, put tomorrow in its place and treasure the day at hand.

Why are there forty days in Lent? It took forty days for sinfulness to drown in the flood before a new creation could inherit the earth. It took forty years for the generation of slaves to die before the freeborn could enter the promised land. For forty days Moses and Elijah and Jesus fasted and prayed to prepare themselves for a life's work.

At the beginning of Lent the bishop calls out the names of the catechumens who seek to be baptized at Easter. Their names are written in the book of the elect, the chosen. God has chosen them, and they have chosen to turn to God. Lent is the forty days before the baptism of the catechumens. The already baptized can share the excitement and the struggles of the elect and rediscover the meaning of baptism in their own lives. During the forty days, both catechumens and the faithful journey together to the holy font.

We keep Lent together. We put aside our business-as-usual to support each other in prayer, fasting and almsgiving. We turn to God to enlighten us and purify us throughout the lengthening brightness of our holy season of Lent.

"For now is the acceptable time! Now is the day of salvation!"

34

Lenten Fast and Abstinence:
An Invitation to Awareness

"What are you hungry for?" Sometimes the answer is obvious: pizza, Chinese food, a juicy steak. Our spiritual hungers are rarely that easy to identify. The season of Lent, our 40-day preparation for Easter, is our annual invitation to grow in awareness of those deeper hungers. We need Lent to help us recognize that our meaning and mission are rooted in Jesus' dying and rising. Together with those preparing for baptism, we join in outward signs of our inner conversion. Our year-round prayer, fasting and almsgiving take on new meaning during this season.

Catholics were once well known for their practice of not eating meat on Friday — a specific form of fasting called abstinence. Stories abound of the lengths Catholics would go to keep this law. Of course, as with any law, it was not that difficult to meet the letter of the law and violate its spirit. One might enjoy a fine lobster dinner or fish fry at a local restaurant and still meet the law's requirements. Catholics were also called to limit their food intake on a variety of other fast days. The reforms which followed the Second Vatican Council sought to simplify the often complicated questions that arose regarding fast and abstinence while re-emphasizing the continuing need for such

practices. The current laws took effect in 1966. They read simply: "Catholics who have celebrated their 14th birthday are bound to abstain from meat on Ash Wednesday and each Friday of Lent. Catholics who have celebrated their 18th birthday, in addition to abstaining from meat, should fast, i.e., eat only one full meal on Ash Wednesday and Good Friday. Smaller quantities of food may be taken at two other meals but no food should be consumed at any other time during those two days. The obligation of fasting ceases with the celebration of one's 59th birthday."

The spirit of the law may invite us to fast from other activities as well: from television or computer games, from eating out or from gossiping. These minimum requirements make the most sense when they are combined with prayer and almsgiving. These age-old disciplines reflect our most fundamental concerns: our relationship with God (prayer), with our bodies (fasting) and with each other (almsgiving).

35

Triduum

A Sense of the Season

The word *Triduum* comes from the Latin and means "three days." It is commonly pronounced "TRIH-doo-uhm" and is usually used in reference to the Easter Triduum, the three most sacred days in the church year. The Easter Triduum begins with the evening Mass of the Lord's Supper on Holy Thursday, reaches its high point at the Easter Vigil and concludes with evening prayer on Easter Sunday. Often there is confusion about how that block of time can be counted as three days. The traditional Jewish practice of counting days from sunset to sunset is used during the Triduum. Thus, Holy Thursday evening to Good Friday evening is the first day, Good Friday evening to Holy Saturday evening is the second day and Holy Saturday evening to Sunday evening is the third day. After centuries of neglect, Pope Pius XII in 1955 restored the Triduum liturgies to their rightful place as the culmination of the entire liturgical year.

Although we talk of the three days, our Triduum prayer is best understood as one liturgy in three interlocking movements. The death and resurrection of the Lord cannot be separated. The meaning of these days is distorted when we imagine that the liturgy re-enacts the final events in the life of Jesus in a sort of historical review. We miss the point in that case. The mystery of Jesus' death and resurrection is a present reality; the boundaries of time, and the boundaries of death, have no power here.

Our past, present and future are irrevocably marked by our own immersion into this mystery through baptism. We wash one another's feet, reverence the cross, light fires in the night and proclaim the stories of our salvation with an awed awareness that this is what it means to be baptized. The Easter Vigil then is the premier time to welcome new members into the church through baptism, confirmation and Eucharist.

Ideally, no other parish events are scheduled on these three days; the presence, time and energy of every person in the community are needed for what we do here. Yes, this may be inconvenient, but birth and death are rarely convenient! Our forty days of prayer, fasting and almsgiving lead us to the Triduum — beyond its history, into its mystery.

36

The Pillar of Fire

What is this great paschal candle that stands in our midst, that during the Fifty Days of Easter seems always to be burning, never to go out?

It is the pillar of fire by which God led the children of Israel from slavery to freedom, through the dusty desert to the land flowing with milk and honey. Behind it, we marched freed from sin from the gloom of exile back into our church's house on Easter's eve. With it, we led those chosen for the sacraments of new life to the font of baptism that is both tomb and womb.

It is the holy sign of Christ our Light. (Thanks be to God!) On it, we traced the sign of Christ yesterday and today, the beginning and the end, the alpha and omega. Into it, we pressed five jewels that are the wounds of divine hands and feet and side. For it, we sang our song of consecration and praise: "Accept, O God, this Easter candle. Let it shine with the lights of heaven and bravely burn forever!" From it, we take our own light, a flame divided but undimmed. All who are baptized walk in its glow.

For fifty days it shines gloriously in the assembly of the church. Then, held in a place of honor near the font, it is brought out and lit for every evening sacrifice of praise, for every baptism and every funeral, every birth and every birth unto eternal life. And as the days and seasons turn, slowly this pillar of finest wax and strongest wick is consumed, burned down, eaten up by fire, sacrificed — like Christ himself — and never truly extinguished. And so it measures our days and seasons until it is Easter again, until once more we sing in the light of a new paschal candle: "May the Morning Star which never sets find this flame still burning: Christ the Morning Star, who came back from the dead and shed his peaceful light on all people." Thanks be to God!

37

Eastertime

A Sense of the Season

First, we kept the forty days, with praying, fasting and giving alms. Then we celebrated the three days of Christ's passion, dying and rising. Now we delight in the fifty days, with rejoicing, feasting and giving witness! The season of Easter is fifty days long. It is a time of unbridled joy, of exuberant rejoicing. The church tells us, "The fifty days from Easter Sunday to Pentecost are celebrated in joyful exultation as one feast day, or better as one 'great Sunday.' These above all others are days for the singing of the Alleluia." (*General Norms for the Liturgical Year and Calendar*, #22)

Why is Eastertime fifty days? The ancient cultures that gave us the Bible had great respect for numbers. They believed that numbers contained hints about God and the meaning of life. The number seven was thought to contain fullness: There are seven days in the week, according to God's original way of ordering time, creating all that there is and resting. So if you multiply 7 times 7, you have "fullness times fullness."

But wait! 7×7 is 49! With God, there is always more — more than we can ever imagine. So our holy season of Easter is even more than "fullness times fullness." It's "fullness times fullness" and then some: $7 \times 7 + 1$. That's what love is like: more than we can ever imagine. That's what heaven is going to be like: more than we can ever imagine.

The fifty days are days for looking for the risen Lord among us, for hearing in each other's stories of rising from the big and small deaths, days when we experience something of Christ's triumphs. That's why we look to the newly baptized, robed in bright new clothes and oily with gladness: At Easter, they died and rose with Christ! Now they take their places with us. Together, like the apostles who were so full of the Spirit that people thought they were drunk, we rush about with good and giddy news: Death is not the last word! Life and love are forever! And slowly, painstakingly, we work together, together with Christ, to change this world into the world to come. Sing Alleluia!

38

Ordinary Time: Summer

A Sense of the Season

What do the words *Ordinary Time* mean? Dorothy Day said, "The words 'Ordinary Time' in our prayer books put me in a state of confusion and irritation. To me, no time is ordinary." She was right. The *Ordinary* in "Ordinary Time" refers to ordinal — counted — time, not to a lack of something to celebrate. The Roman document, *General Norms for the Liturgical Year and Calendar,* says: "Apart from those seasons having their own distinctive character [Advent, Christmastime, Lent, Triduum and Eastertime], 33 or 34 weeks remain in the yearly cycle that do not celebrate a specific aspect of the mystery of Christ. Rather, especially on the Sundays, they are devoted to the mystery of Christ in all its aspects."

How do we celebrate "the mystery of Christ in all its aspects"? We gather every Sunday. Sunday is our original feast day. Christians have gathered every Sunday — the day of Christ's resurrection, the first day of the week — ever since there were Christians.

When we gather on Sundays in Ordinary Time, as always, we hear the scriptures proclaimed. The church reads straight through "the gospel of the year," either Matthew, Mark or Luke, each week often picking up where we left off last week. (We read John during Lent and Easter, and on feasts.) The first readings, from the first testament of the Bible, have been chosen for their relationship to the gospel passages. Many voices are heard throughout summer Ordinary Time. We also read through some of the letters of the second testament of the Bible. The mystery of Christ "in all its aspects" unfolds.

What is the heart of our Sunday celebration? We do our eucharist; that is, we do our thanksgiving. We praise and thank God for all creation; we pray for the whole world, as we remember Christ's life, death and resurrection. We share the bread and wine, the body and blood. We are sent forth to be the body and blood of Christ in our homes, our workplaces, our neighborhoods, our towns, our cities, our country, our world.

"What happens in our churches every Sunday is the fruit of our week. What happens as the fruit of the week past is the beginning of the week to come. Sunday is simultaneously a point of arrival and departure for Christians on their way to the fullness of the kingdom. This is not ordinary at all. This is the fabric of Christian living." (*Saint Andrew Bible Missal* [Brooklyn: William J. Hirten Co., 1982.])

39

Ordinary Time: Autumn

A Sense of the Season

All of our days are numbered. Now that Christ has risen from the dead and ascended into heaven, we count down the days until he returns in glory to judge the living and the dead. *Ordinary Time* is "ordinal" time: numbered days, days in which we lay out the scriptures and the prayers to bide our time until Christ returns.

Although the church makes no official distinction between the days of Ordinary Time from Pentecost until Advent, in our lives we experience the subtle shift from the relaxed days of summer to the increasingly active days of autumn. For some of us, the shift comes with the end-of-summer holiday or the beginning of school. Others see work activities shift, from tending to harvesting, from stocking shelves to increasing sales, from cashing out an old fiscal year to digging into a new one.

The church's calendar contains some subtle shifts, too. On September 14 we celebrate the Holy Cross, and the waning of the natural world around us points us to the mystery of suffering and redemption. At the end of September we invoke the holy archangels to guard us in the encroaching twilight. And if we listen closely to the scriptures in October, we begin to hear talk of the last days and the final things. These thoughts reach their culmination with the great festival of saints and souls, November 1 and 2. And we spend November remembering the dead, preparing for the end and celebrating Christ, the firstfruits harvested of the new creation, the firstborn from the dead.

This is the extraordinary opportunity that autumn's Ordinary Time opens up for us.

40

The Ascension of the Lord

Great feast that Easter is, one day (not even three days!) is insufficient to celebrate the fullness of the mystery of the resurrection. So, as Christians, we keep a fifty-day-long festival, punctuated by the Solemnity of the Ascension of our Lord — the fortieth day of Easter. The feast of the Ascension, like a prism, helps us focus the wondrous colors of the Easter spectrum.

These images from the Ascension liturgy give us a sense of the hope and joy that color this feast: "Christ's ascension is our glory and hope." "The joy of the resurrection and the ascension renews the whole world." "Where Christ has gone, we hope to follow." "Christ has passed beyond our sight, not to abandon us, but to be our hope." "Christ was taken up to heaven to claim for us a share in his divine life."

If we have been united with Christ through baptism in his death and resurrection, we are surely united with him in the transformation and redemption of his humanity. What we celebrate, however, is not only a past or future event. We are given glimpses of our glorious destiny even now. So, feet firmly planted on earth, the community gathers to rejoice in the life we share with the risen Lord.

41

Celebrating the Human Body

August 15

The Solemnity of the Assumption is the oldest and greatest feast of Mary. Orthodox Christians call August 15 the Dormition ("falling asleep") of Mary.

"She who sheltered the Divine Word in her breast was to be lodged in the dwelling place of her Son," says Saint John Damascene, describing his belief that after Mary's death, her body was raised to live with God forever. That Mary's body — not just her soul — is in God's presence is a sign of the holiness of creation. The human body is not evil — it is good. Death is not the end of creation — it is the beginning of eternal life. In our day, when violence can desecrate the human body, the sign of Mary's assumption gains new import.

The New Testament reading for this feast calls Jesus the firstfruits of those who have died, to be followed by the harvest of all who hope in him. As Mary, the model believer and sign of the church, is gathered in, we hope that we too will one day be part of this harvest. We surround Mary's statue at church and at home with brilliant clusters of flowers, herbs and fruits — the first harvest of our gardens.

42

All Saints' Day

November 1

Today we keep the festival of your holy city,
the heavenly Jerusalem, our mother.
Around your throne
the saints, our brothers and sisters,
sing your praise for ever.
Their glory fills us with joy,
and their communion with us in your church
gives us inspiration and strength
as we hasten on our pilgrimage of faith,
eager to meet them.

So we pray during the Mass of All Saints. We celebrate those who have made the long journey to the holy city, to Jerusalem, to the feast of heaven. The scriptures and prayers for the day tell us that we are part of that vast throng now standing before God's throne in ceaseless praise. From the second reading: "I saw before me a huge crowd which no one could count from every nation, race, people and tongue . . . dressed in long white robes." At our baptism, when we received our white robes, we became part of this great assembly. Indeed, every time we go to Mass, before we sing Holy, Holy, we recall that we sing God's praise with "angels and archangels and the whole company of heaven."

Who is this company and why is it so wonderful to be part of it? This is another way of asking, "What does the communion of saints mean?" It is not complicated. All the baptized, living and dead, across the generations, walk together, suffer together, sing together — not only those who have died, and not only those who lead heroic lives. Vincent Harding, writing in *Sojourners* magazine, put it this way: "What a wild company we belong to! These are wild people, persecuted people, going-out, not-knowing-where-they're-going people." For a picture of what the lives of saints look like, read the Beatitudes (Matthew 5:1–12.)

43

All Souls

November 2

Because we know that death is not the end of life, it is not morbid for us Christians to visit the graves of our loved ones who have died. It is good to visit the cemetery, especially on November 2 and then throughout the month of November, when the church celebrates the communion of saints and souls and looks forward to that harvest at the end of time when all will be gathered into the new Jerusalem.

We decorate the graves of our loved ones because we believe that in baptism they have died with Christ and thus Christ will raise them up. So we place on the grave an evergreen wreath — the ancient crown of victory over death and a reminder of the eternal life promised to us in the first sacrament. Or we light vigil candles on the grave, keeping one lit throughout November — a reflection of the light of Christ given to each one of us on our baptism day, and a reminder of the wise bridesmaids who kept their lamps lit while waiting for the groom to come so that the wedding could begin.

Remember Mary Magdalene and the other two Marys going to visit Jesus' tomb. Confident that what they found, you will one day find, make pilgrimages to the graves of your loved ones this month. Pray at each grave:

Eternal rest grant unto <u>Name</u>, O Lord,
and let perpetual light shine upon <u>her/him</u>.
May <u>she/he</u> rest in peace.
May <u>her/his</u> soul, and the souls
*   of all the faithful departed,*
through the mercy of God,
*   rest in peace. Amen.*

44

Q&A: No Obligation

Why is the obligation to participate at Mass waived on certain holy days?

It can indeed be confusing to determine which holy days are bound by which rules. Simply put, there are six holy days of obligation for most dioceses of the United States: Christmas (December 25), Mary, Mother of God (January 1), Ascension (sixth Thursday after Easter in most places; in some dioceses Ascension is moved to the seventh Sunday of Easter), Assumption (August 15), All Saints (November 1) and Immaculate Conception (December 8). Latin-rite Catholics in the United States are normally obligated to participate at Mass on these days and to refrain from tasks that might limit a joyful celebration of the day.

But there is an exception to the rules. When August 15, November 1 or January 1 falls on a Saturday or Monday, the obligation to attend Mass is no longer in force. The feast remains a significant day in the life of the church, but the obligation to participate at Mass is gone. This policy was approved by the bishops of the United States and confirmed by the Vatican. It went into effect on January 1, 1993.

There are several reasons the bishops chose to remove the obligation to attend Mass on these three holy days. Because of the popularity of vigil or anticipated masses, there is often widespread confusion about which Mass satisfies which obligation when holy days fall on a Monday or Saturday. Furthermore, it is difficult to prepare and celebrate two major feasts back-to-back. In areas where there is a limited number of clergy, the logistics of scheduling become even more of a problem. Finally, it was noted that common practice was to attend either the Sunday celebration or the holy day Mass, but not both.

The observances of holy days are different in different countries. Latin-rite Catholics in the United States observe more holy days than many other countries. But even within this country, practice varies. In nine western states, the feast of the Ascension has been transferred to the following Sunday. Catholics in Hawaii, following the practice of their neighbors in the South Pacific, observe all Sundays and two additional feasts, Christmas and the Immaculate Conception, as holy days of obligation.

45

Nuestra Señora de Guadalupe

December 12

In Advent of 1531, an Aztec peasant named Juan Diego (whose birth name in the Náhuatl language was Cuautlatohua) saw an astounding sight — a radiant woman clothed in the stars, with the moon at her feet. She bore the appearance of a Central American Indian, and she was dressed in native garb. She even wore the traditional sash of a pregnant woman. This was a paradoxical image, for at the time when the Lady of Guadalupe manifested herself, the Indian people were deeply oppressed by their Spanish conquerors. Their everyday experience was one of profound powerlessness. Indian women, especially, were treated cruelly.

The woman spoke to Juan Diego tenderly, calling him her beloved son. The peasant went to his bishop, but the bishop did not think it possible that the Queen of Heaven would appear to a poor man on a barren hillside. As a sign of her presence for the skeptical bishop, the Lady left her glorious image on Juan Diego's cloak of agave cactus cloth. At her request, a church was built at the site where she had appeared — near modern-day Mexico City. Pilgrims come from many nations to honor her there, especially on her feast day, December 12.

The oppressed native people recognized Nuestra Señora de Guadalupe as a promise of justice and a cause for hope. Peace treaties have been signed in the basilica that bears her name. She is the patron saint of Mexico, and she is honored throughout the Americas.

46

Bless Your Door on Epiphany

The gospel tells us that the magi found Christ "on entering the house." The door to your home is a holy threshold. You can bless those who come in and go out by inscribing above the door in chalk the first two numbers of the year + C + M + B + the last two numbers of the year. Tradition tells us that the letters stand for the names of the magi: Caspar, Melchior and Balthasar. Adolph Adam points out that it may also mean *"Christus mansionem benedicat"* or "May Christ bless this dwelling." It's appropriate to bless your door in January — *janua* means "door" and the first month is the door to the new year.

After inscribing the doorway, say this prayer:

God of Bethlehem and Cana,
    God of Jordan's leaping waters,
    in baptism you bring us
        into your family.
You wed us and embrace us
    as your beloved.
May we fill this place
    with kindness to one another,
    with hospitality to guests,
    and with abundant care
        for every stranger.
By the gentle light of a star,
    guide home all who seek you
        on paths of faith, hope and love.
Then we will join the angels in
        proclaiming your praise:
Glory in heaven and peace on earth,
    now and for ever. Amen.
Then sing a Christmas carol.

47

Martin Luther King Day

Here is a way to gather your household to pray on this day.

Leader: God of our work and of our rest, again and again your creatures take sides against one another. Oppression and violence are our sad inheritance. But we still look for you where the lowly are raised up, where the mighty are brought down. We find you in your servants, and we give you thanks for the witness and work of Martin Luther King, Jr. Fill us with a spirit and strength like his, so that day by day we may see where our community is torn by repression and fear and ignorance, and so give ourselves to healing. We make this prayer in the name of Jesus Christ our Lord. Amen.

Reader: Listen now to a reading from the prophet Isaiah. Let these ancient words come to life in memories of Dr. King, who was able to look at sorrow and trouble and yet tell of his dreams of a just society. *(Read Isaiah 62:1–5.)*

The following questions may be used to guide a discussion.

1. How does the Isaiah reading remind us of Dr. King's life and work?

2. What do I know of the world he wanted to change? What do I remember thinking about Dr. King and his followers?

3. Much has changed since Dr. King's time. Much has not, and some things have grown worse. When I look into my own heart, what do I think of the racism that is still there? What sort of stereotypes still exist?

4. What did we learn from Dr. King about suffering and nonviolence, about changing

unjust laws, about the connection between war and racism, about the connection between justice and peace?

After the discussion, the leader can invite all to join in prayer and intercession. All may add prayers of their own.

Leader: Help us, Lord, to draw strength from the words and vision of Martin Luther King. *(silence)* Give us courage, God, to face the unfair judgments we make of other races, other cultures, other ways of life. Give us the willingness to be fair. *(silence)* Show us, O God, how to be the church of Jesus: always facing up to injustice, speaking for the silent, calling the world from violence.

To conclude, the leader can invite all to pray the Lord's Prayer. The song, "We shall overcome," closely associated with Dr. King's life, could be sung.

This material originally appeared in the 1986 packet from the National Catholic Conference for Interracial Justice, and is reprinted here with permission. Art by Rita Corbin.

Saint Blase Blessing

February 3

Sickness and suffering are mysteries that confront most Christians at some time in their lives. Believers cherish the stories of Jesus' tender concern for the poor and sick who sought to find relief and meaning in their struggles. The flesh-and-blood example of a long line of Christian witnesses whose faith sustained them in time of trial offers us hope when shadows darken our lives. Saint Blase was such a person.

Blase served as bishop of Armenia in the fourth century. Little is known about his life, but tradition tells us that he saved a small boy from choking on a fish bone. Because of this, his help is sought for those who are sick, especially those who are afflicted with illnesses of the throat. On February 3, the feast of Saint Blase, the church continues its ministry to the sick with the blessing of throats.

This blessing, which can take place either after the homily at Mass or as part of a liturgy of the word, invokes God's healing and protection. Two blessed candles, joined in the form of a cross, are placed around the throat of each person seeking a blessing. The minister then prays, "Through the intercession of Saint Blase, bishop and martyr, may God deliver you from every disease of the throat and from every other illness: In the name of the Father, and of the Son, and of the Holy Spirit." Humbled by physical weakness and human limitations, we acknowledge our faith in God's protective love for all who call upon God's name.

49

Charles Lwanga and Companions

June 3

It was not until late in the nineteenth century that Christian missionaries began to preach the word of God in central Africa. The missionaries had some initial success, but when a ruler named Mwanga rose to power, the lives of the believers were threatened. Those closest to the king were most at risk. When the leader of the court's pages was put to death for his beliefs, the other pages were inspired, not terrified, by his martyrdom. Charles Lwanga became the new leader of the pages. He instructed the young men about Christian beliefs and encouraged them to stand firm against the king's immorality.

The evil king was enraged by the pages' refusal to cooperate with him. He called them all together and demanded that anyone who was a Christian step forward and admit their loyalty to Christ. Courageously, Charles and his companions came forward. The king immediately had them imprisoned. There they were beaten and starved while they waited for the soldiers to prepare a funeral pyre for their execution. Charles continued to urge his companions to be faithful to Christian teachings. On June 3, 1886, the young men, all under the age of 25, were wrapped in reed mats and burned on a pyre. Charles Lwanga and his companions were the first martyrs of central Africa.

The king's intention was to stamp out Christianity, but the young men's courage and unshakable faith in the face of death had precisely the opposite effect. Within a year, the number of Christians who were baptized or preparing for baptism as catechumens had more than doubled. Today there are over six million Christians in Uganda, proving what one of the martyrs said after his arrest, "When we are gone, others will rise in our place." Pope Paul VI canonized Charles and his companions in 1964. We remember them every year on June 3.

Copyright © 1997 Archdiocese of Chicago: Liturgy Training Publications, 1800 North Hermitage Avenue, Chicago IL 60622-1101; 1-800-933-1800. Text by Kathy Luty. Art by Chuck Ludeke.

50

Apostles Peter and Paul

June 29

One of the oldest saints' days in Rome, June 29 was dedicated to the memory of the apostles Peter and Paul as early as the fourth century. This day the church remembers two disciples who differed greatly in style and background, but who shared a tireless energy in spreading the gospel.

Rough-hewn and impulsive Peter left his fishing nets immediately to answer Jesus' call. Later, during the passion of Jesus, Peter made his denials just as impulsively, though he had pledged his loyalty to Jesus only that evening. Receiving Christ's gracious forgiveness after the resurrection, Peter went on to become the rock-steady and faithful leader of the disciples. Imprisoned three or four times, he eventually was crucified during the reign of Nero. Legend has it that he was hung on the cross head down because he told the soldiers that he was not worthy to die in the same manner as Christ.

Once Paul, who had been a rigid and violent persecutor of Christians, experienced the love of Christ, he grew meek — though never shy. He founded many churches and was able to affirm the fledgling communities of believers even while he was admonishing them. Paul's writings are the first Christian scriptures; they are older than the gospels. After many imprisonments, Paul was executed during the reign of Nero. Since he was a Roman citizen, he was beheaded instead of crucified.

Coastal countries like Chile and Paraguay remember Peter the fisherman with nautical parades. In Hungary and in rural England, people braid straw from the wheat harvest into crosses and crowns to honor the two martyr saints.

51

Blessed Kateri Tekakwitha

July 14

What heroic deeds cause us to remember Kateri Tekakwitha, who died at the age of 24, only seven years after she was baptized? Kateri was born in upstate New York in 1656. Her mother, a Christian Algonquin, and her father, a Mohawk warrior, died of smallpox when Kateri was four. Kateri survived the epidemic but was left disfigured and partially blind. She grew up in the care of her uncle.

When Kateri was eleven, a group of Jesuit missionaries (called "Blackrobes" by the native peoples) visited Kateri's village. Their stories touched her deeply. At the age of 17, she took the courageous step of being baptized. Her decision to be baptized angered her relatives. They knew of so-called Christians who had burned villages and brought deadly diseases to the Native American peoples. Kateri also chose not to marry, which was unthinkable for a young girl in her culture.

The opposition of her relatives to her choices led Kateri to flee to a Christian settlement near Montreal. There she taught young children and cared for the sick and aged. She quickly became known for her remarkable acts of penance and prayer. But soon her health began to fail. She died in 1680 at the age of 24.

Because she followed the traditional Christian virtues of prayer, fasting and works of mercy to such an extraordinary degree, it was not long before word of her life spread far and wide. Kateri was beatified, a preliminary step for sainthood, in 1980. She is the first Native American and the first American lay person to receive this honor. We honor the "Lily of the Mohawks" each year on July 14.

52

The Triumph of the Cross

September 14

September 14 is the feast of the Triumph of the Cross, previously called the Exaltation of the Cross. Christians have celebrated this feast on this day since the first half of the fourth century. According to an Eastern text, the empress Helena discovered the Lord's cross on September 14, 320. Fifteen years later, on September 13, two churches on Golgotha in Jerusalem were consecrated (the Church of the Cross and the Church of the Resurrection). On the following day, the relic of the cross found by Helena was

solemnly exposed for public veneration. An annual commemoration began in Jerusalem, and churches in other cities that had relics of the cross brought them forth this day for veneration by the faithful. The ceremony was called the *exaltatio* (lifting up). What follows are some words our ancestors in the faith have used to describe the mystery, glory and power of the cross of Christ.

May I never boast of anything but the cross of our Lord Jesus Christ! Through it, the world has been crucified to me and I to the world.

Galatians 6:14 – 16

Faithful Cross, above all other,
One and only noble tree,
None in foliage, none in blossom,
None in fruit your peer may be;
Sweet the wood and sweet the iron
And your load, most sweet is he.

Bend your boughs, O Tree of glory!
All your rigid branches, bend!
For a while the ancient temper
That your birth bestowed, suspend;
And the King of earth and heaven
Gently on your bosom tend.

Venantius Fortunatus, 6th century

How splendid the cross of Christ!
It brings life, not death; light, not darkness;
Paradise, not its loss. It is the wood on
which the Lord, like a great warrior, was
wounded in hands and feet and side, but
healed thereby our wounds. A tree had
destroyed us, a tree now brought us life.

Theodore of Studios, 9th century

53

Andrew Dung-Lac and Companions

November 24

Andrew Dung-Lac was a Vietnamese-born priest who, along with more than 100 other Christians, was martyred for his faith during a time of religious persecution in 19th-century Vietnam. Catholicism had been introduced into Vietnam by Jesuit missionaries; they had opened a permanent mission in Da Nang as early as 1615. Andrew was the son of Buddhist parents who allowed him to be instructed in the Catholic faith.

It was dangerous to be a Christian at that time, but that did not stop Andrew from working as a catechist, teaching others about the faith. Eventually he decided to become a priest; Andrew was nearly 40 years old when he was ordained. During one of the many persecutions, Andrew was arrested. His parishioners collected the money needed to free him. Not long after, a law was passed requiring all citizens to help in the building of temples and to participate in ancestor worship. Many Christians, Andrew among them, refused to obey the new law. Andrew was arrested again. He was beheaded in 1839 because he would not renounce his Catholic faith. In the years between 1820 and 1862, 8 bishops, 50 priests and 59 lay persons were put to death because of their belief in Jesus. This group included French, Spanish and Vietnamese missionaries.

Pope John Paul II recognized the powerful witness of these Christian martyrs when he canonized them in June 1988. Because of their courage, the church in Vietnam continues to spread the good news of the gospel in our own day. We remember Andrew Dung-Lac and his companions on November 24.

54

Going to a Wedding

Weddings are often occasions when people of different traditions or even different faiths gather. Actively participating in wedding ceremonies of other traditions or faiths — singing, saying the prayers, making the gestures — may not be easy if we are unfamiliar with them.

But have you noticed that even at a wedding Mass where most of the people are Catholic, the singing is poor, the responses to the presider or lector lack enthusiasm and people are slow to stand, sit or walk in procession at the appropriate times? Why is this? Even with the addition of the marriage vows and exchange of rings after the homily, the shape of the wedding Mass is that of Sunday eucharist, a sacred deed that we are very accustomed to doing. Even when a wedding is celebrated according to the rite of marriage "outside of Mass," it still has the familiar structure of the liturgy of the word — the first part of Mass. Why then, at a wedding, do we often act as if it's the first time we've ever been to church?

Maybe the excitement of the occasion or the stress of the many details that go into a big family celebration distract us. If the wedding is at another parish, maybe the music is unfamiliar. Or maybe the musicians are performers rather than leaders. Whatever the causes, the unfortunate result is that we often miss a unique opportunity to do what we are called to do always and everywhere: give thanks and praise to God as the body of Christ. We miss an opportunity to bless the new husband and wife by thanking God with and for them, praising God for their love for each other, which is a sure sign of the love God has for us.

So if you'll be attending a wedding soon, promise yourself that you won't miss the opportunity to praise and thank God. Even though you may be seated by an usher from the wedding party, move in close to the other people around you to create a sense of community. Introduce yourself to any strangers seated around you.

Stand and sit promptly so that the presider doesn't say, "Please stand now for the gospel," or "Be seated." Don't distract others — or yourself — by fiddling with cameras. (Take pictures after Mass or at the reception.) Make your responses enthusiastically: "Amen!" "And also with you!" "Thanks be to God!" "It is right to give God thanks and praise!"

And most importantly, sing out. Sing as though the future health and happiness of the new couple depended on it. Because in a sense, it does. More supportive than the toaster or towels that you give as a gift, a good liturgy is the best beginning for a Christian marriage. And the beginning of good liturgy is our full, conscious and active participation in it. Lift up your hearts!

Q&A: Another Wedding

What does it mean to "convalidate" a marriage?

We probably all know at least one couple who were not married according to the legal requirements of the Catholic church. Perhaps the couple were married in a civil ceremony. Or maybe they were married in the church of the non-Catholic partner without having gone through the procedure of receiving a dispensation from the Catholic church. Perhaps one of the partners had been married previously and was not at the time of the new marriage canonically free to marry again.

It is not unusual for such couples to wish later to have the Catholic church formally recognize their marriage. They are encouraged to discuss their situation with their pastor and explore the possibility of *convalidating* their marriage. Convalidation is the process by which the church recognizes a marriage that did not previously meet the requirements of canon law.

In a simple validation process, a couple in a stable marriage participates in some form of preparation, and then renews their consent — "I do" — in the presence of a priest or deacon and two witnesses. This renewal may take place with as much or as little ceremony as the couple and their pastor decide is right for them.

Each couple's circumstances differ, of course, calling for different procedures. In any event, the process of convalidating a marriage respects the needs of each couple as well as the teachings of the Catholic church. Through it, the couple's experience of married love is interpreted in a new context — the paschal mystery — the pattern at the heart of every Christian marriage.

56

Anointing of the Sick I: The Mystery of Illness

We get hurt. We wear out. The lungs, the eyes, the memory, and any of the many limbs and organs that compose us break or ache. Gloom comes over us then: pity for ourselves, sorrow, depression, anger. But hope can come, too, and courage, and sometimes peace.

All of this is marked and celebrated in the rites of our tradition. With a word and a deed, with touch and breath and spit and mud, Jesus heals those who ail. In every place and time, we who are the church remember and tell stories of healing, anoint the sick with oil and share the one bread even with those who cannot assemble for Mass. Thus the sick and the healthy, the homebound and the spry, saints and sinners are made one and remain one, a single body of many parts.

Anyone who is seriously ill can be anointed, including the elderly who become weaker, even if no illness is present; those waiting for surgery when a serious condition is the reason for the operation; sick children who have sufficient use of reason to be helped by the celebration; and those who are unconscious or who have lost the use of reason, provided that they probably would have asked for the sacrament had they the use of their faculties. Furthermore, many forms of mental illness are now known to be serious. So the mentally ill may be anointed, provided that they will be helped and not harmed by the rite. If you have questions, consult a priest or other parish leader.

The most complete celebration of the sacrament is a communal one, a celebration in which those to be anointed are surrounded and supported by other members of the Christian community, whether at home, or in the house of the church (for those who can leave their beds and come here). In song and in silence, with scriptures and prayers, we strengthen the bonds of love and faith that are stronger than the most lethal disease and more powerful even than death.

57

Anointing of the Sick II: Celebrating the Sacrament

The sacrament of the anointing of the sick is a celebration in which those who are seriously ill or infirm are surrounded and supported by other members of the Christian community, whether at home or in the house of the church (for those who can leave their beds and come here). In song and in silence, with scriptures and prayers, we strengthen the bonds of love and faith that are stronger than the most lethal disease and more powerful even than death. The sacrament may be celebrated in the context of a Mass, or on its own, depending on the needs of the person who is sick.

The celebration opens with brief introductory rites that help us remember that God is with us and that we are the body of Christ. Then follows a liturgy of the word, in which we hear scriptures that shed light on the meaning of sickness and suffering and the compassion of our God, who suffers with us. Depending on the needs of the person who is sick, one brief passage or two or three readings and a psalm may be used. A homily may be preached, too.

Then the rite continues. The gathered church surrounds the person who is sick with the prayer of faith. In response to God's word, a litany is prayed. Then, the priest does the laying on of hands, an ancient sign of the moving of the Holy Spirit to heal and save. This is done in silence. Then a prayer is said over the oil of the sick. Finally, the priest anoints the head and the hands, and sometimes other parts of the body (the feet, for example, or the part of the body that is in pain) of the one who is sick. While anointing the sick person's head, the priest says "Through this holy anointing, may the Lord in his love and mercy help you with the grace of the Holy Spirit." And all answer "Amen!" While anointing the hands, the priest says, "May the Lord who frees you from sin save you and raise you up." And again, all answer "Amen!" If other parts of the body are anointed, no words are said. A final prayer is then said.

The liturgy of the eucharist, or simply the giving of communion, may follow. Or the rite ends with a blessing. If you or someone you know is in need of the anointing, please call the parish office.

58

Communion Call

As early as the year 150, the martyr Justin, in writing an explanation of Christian worship to the Roman authorities, described the Sunday eucharist pretty much as we celebrate it today. At the end of the description, he notes that ministers take the eucharist from the Sunday assembly to those who were unable to be present. Perhaps these included people who were in prison for living according to the gospel, and those whose work (Sunday was a work day back then) kept them away. But almost certainly he meant the sick and the infirm, and those who were otherwise homebound. This is our ancient tradition: to love and cherish and to keep connected with those members of this community who cannot be with us on Sunday.

When illness or infirmity keeps you from the Sunday assembly, ministers of communion will bring a word of scripture and the body of Christ to you. Call the parish office and we will set this up. The best time for this is Sunday, when the minister can come straight from the celebration of Mass. But other times can be arranged. Don't worry about fasting before receiving communion: If you are able to, that's fine. But because of your condition, you are not obligated.

The rite of communion for the sick is simple. It can be very brief if you are not feeling up to more. But normally, it consists of some opening prayers and readings (similar to those at Mass). If you are able, you then offer some prayers for the world and the church. Your family, friends and caregivers can (and should!) participate in the rite. If they would normally receive communion at Mass, then they can share in communion at this time, too. Before and after this simple, powerful rite of communion, you can visit with the minister or not, depending on how you feel.

Sick or infirm, homebound or hospitalized, each baptized person is nonetheless part of this parish, a member of the body of Christ. So don't be afraid that you're being a burden, and don't think that we're so busy we wouldn't have time for you. Regularly sharing in communion is an important part of our life together as the church.

59

Communion of the Dying

We used to think that the anointing was our "last rites" — "extreme unction" we called it. But we know that you don't have to be dying to be anointed. The strong grace of the sacrament of the anointing is available to all who are seriously sick.

So what are our "last rites"? Our last rite is our every-Sunday rite: holy communion. When holy communion is shared with the dying, it is called *viaticum*. This is a Latin word that means "food to go with you on the way." The bread of life, the cup of eternal salvation — these are our final nourishment on this earth, and our promise of safe passover to the next. Jesus said that those who eat of this bread and drink of this cup have life to the full.

The most complete form of viaticum is to celebrate Mass at the bedside of the dying Christian. Since that is not always possible, communion can be brought from a celebration of Mass back at the parish church. The rite of communion of the dying is easy to follow, and it can be brief when necessary. It is best done with the participation of other parishioners, family members and friends, and even those caregivers present who may wish to join in. Depending on the condition of the dying Christian, there may be singing, and there will be a reading (maybe two) from scriptures, prayers, including the Lord's Prayer, and times for silent reflection. Anyone who normally could receive communion at Mass is welcome to share in the eucharist at viaticum, too — a sure sign of our oneness in Christ, a love that is stronger than death.

60

Order of Christian Funerals I:
The Vigil

The vigil (or wake) service is the first of the three primary rites of the Catholic funeral liturgy. Along with the funeral liturgy itself and the rite of committal, these rites mark significant moments for the mourners as they come to terms with the loss of their loved one. Frequently, the vigil is the first public gathering of the deceased's family and friends — an acknowledgment of the reality of the death when it feels so unreal. This time of keeping watch in the presence of the deceased is an invitation to share the memories that forged the bond between the deceased and the mourners. It includes both formal and informal opportunities for all to express their sense of loss and grief.

It is in this context that the church invites mourners to recall "God's designs for a world in which suffering and death will relinquish their hold on all whom God has called his own." In the words of the scriptures and through prayers of intercession for both the deceased and mourners, the church reminds us that death is not the last word. Music plays an integral role in this rite, touching unspoken dimensions of both feeling and faith. Sung prayer allows the mourners to hear the faith that surrounds them. A priest, deacon, lay minister or even a family member may lead the prayer at the vigil.

This more formal vigil service may be preceded or followed by the recitation of the rosary or other devotions, if these prayers have special meaning for the gathered community.

Cultural practices are changing regarding funeral services. Certain elements are sometimes telescoped, resulting in one major liturgical moment (often the funeral liturgy) with an abridged time of vigil immediately before the liturgy or perhaps a private interment the next day. Christians are challenged to balance carefully what is lost and what is gained by these practices. The options chosen should respect the wishes of the deceased. But in a sense, funeral rites are for the survivors and so should best serve the mourners and the faith community.

61

Order of Christian Funerals II:
The Funeral Liturgy

Through its ministry at the time of death, the church shows reverence for the body of the deceased and offers comfort and hope to the mourners. The funeral liturgy is the central celebration of the church at the hour of death. Because of this, the funeral liturgy should be scheduled at a time when as many members of the Christian community as possible can be present.

The celebration of a funeral Mass is most appropriate because it is our primary experience of the death and resurrection of Jesus. The Mass is ordinarily celebrated in the parish church. It is here that believers are welcomed into the Christian community and nourished with the body and blood of Christ. It is fitting that the body of the deceased be returned to the church to be commended to the Lord.

The funeral Mass begins with the reception of the body at the door of the church. The casket is sprinkled with holy water and clothed with the pall in reminder of baptism. Other Christian symbols may also be placed on the coffin once it is brought to rest in the assembly. The Easter candle burns before the body, silently proclaiming Christ as light in our darkness. It reminds us that in baptism we died with Christ so that we might also live with Christ. Family and friends are nourished with the word of God and the body and blood of Christ. The prayer in church may conclude with a final commendation through which the members of the community entrust their loved one to the tender embrace of God. The song of farewell can express both sadness and hope in eternal life.

Family members can shape the funeral liturgy to reflect the life of the deceased in the context of faith. They may select the scripture reading, psalms, hymns and intercessions that best give voice to their experience of this death and what, in faith, it means. Family members and friends can serve as pallbearers, readers, giftbearers or eucharistic ministers. They may clothe the casket with the pall and offer words of remembrance during the final commendation. No one should be forced to take a role at the funeral liturgy. However, the full and active participation of the gathered community can be a source of comfort and hope in the paschal mystery.

62

Order of Christian Funerals III: The Rite of Committal

The rite of committal is the third major ritual of the Christian community as it accompanies the body of the deceased to its final resting place. The word "final" is all too appropriate for this difficult time of leave-taking. The stark reality of bidding farewell to someone we have loved looms in the moments ahead. The church surrounds the mourners with hope and belief in the power of the resurrection precisely when they most need to hear that message. In no way does faith deny the very painful reality of death and grief; instead it embraces that grief while standing firm in the hope of eternal life.

The rite of committal frequently follows the funeral liturgy. It is to take place whenever possible at the site itself. Note that this does not mean in the cemetery chapel, but at the open grave, in the mausoleum or at the crematorium. This face-to-face encounter with the place of interment goes against our American tendencies to avoid such direct reminders of the reality of death and to express our grief in private. Here at the grave or place of interment, the intense emotions of the mourners may be expressed, secure in the knowledge that the support of the church and family and friends is close at hand. Of course, severe weather or the infirmity of the primary mourners may necessitate that the rite of committal take place in the cemetery chapel. But these — not the convenience of cemetery workers or pastoral leaders — should be the real reason for such an exception.

The rite of committal expresses the communion between the church on earth and the church in heaven as the mourners surrender the body of their loved one into the welcoming embrace of the angels and saints. Accompanied by words of scripture and blessing, the actual interment of the body may take place in the presence of the mourners. This is the core of what we have come to do. In this way the church invites us to see the grave not as a place of despair, but as a sign of hope and promise. A simple gesture such as placing a flower or soil upon the casket, or kissing or sprinkling the casket with holy water may conclude the ritual, serving as the final farewell of the assembly and each person in it.

63

Concerns about Funerals

National flags: Citizens who have earned the right to have their casket draped with their national flag are rightly proud to do so. At a Catholic funeral, the casket may be draped with the flag during the vigil and the rite of committal. In the funeral liturgy, however, the status of the deceased as a child of God by baptism takes precedence. At the door of the church, the flag is replaced by the pall, a reminder of the white garment of baptism. The flag may be replaced after the casket is taken from the church.

Suicide: The death of a loved one by suicide complicates the normal anguish of family and friends after a death. The church offers the full support of its ministers at this difficult time. The funeral liturgy and its related rites are not denied to a person who ended his or her life by suicide. Special prayers are provided in the rite for this circumstance.

Cremation: Although the church recommends that the custom of burying the dead be observed, assuming proper motives, cremation is permissible. The Order of Christian Funerals prefers that cremation take place after the funeral liturgy and before the committal service. The rite of committal includes a prayer specifically for a person who has been cremated. The church prefers that cremated remains be buried, not scattered.

Eulogy: A eulogy is a speech that honors someone who has recently died. Because Christian funeral rites focus not simply on the life of the deceased but rather on God's presence and goodness in that person, a eulogy per se is not permitted. However,

words of remembrance that recall the deceased in the light of his or her faith are certainly appropriate, and may be spoken by a family member or friend during the vigil or final commendation.

Funerals during the Triduum: Funeral Masses may not be celebrated on Holy Thursday, Good Friday, Holy Saturday or Easter Sunday. Several options are available. Families may choose to delay the services until after Easter Sunday. Or they may have a funeral liturgy outside Mass, proceed with the interment, and celebrate a memorial Mass after Easter. In this way, both the needs of the mourners and of the larger church can be taken into account.

64

The Church's Daily Prayer

The manner in which we begin and end each day becomes a lens through which we view the rest of the day. This is no contemporary wisdom. As long as human beings have been around to greet each new sunrise and pause in wonder at the setting of the sun, the need to mark the day's beginning and end has been in our bones.

The church, too, acknowledges the natural rhythms of the day by inviting us to share in the prayer called the *Liturgy of the Hours*. In recent centuries, the Liturgy of the Hours was commonly understood to be the domain of priests and nuns. Readers over forty may recall seeing their parish priests and religious praying what was then called the Divine Office from a book called a breviary. As a result of the Second Vatican Council, the Liturgy of the Hours has been restored to its proper place as an integral part of the church's public prayer for all who have been baptized.

For most of us, the Sunday eucharist is our primary gathering for prayer each week. The Liturgy of the Hours invites us to pause during the course of each day, especially at morning and evening, to offer prayers of praise and petition to the God whose loving care permeates our days. Again, readers may recall praying the morning offering or the angelus, traditional prayers that were closely connected to particular times of day.

In the Liturgy of the Hours, Morning Prayer calls us to offer praise and thanks to God for the wonders of creation and the great mystery of the resurrection. With psalms and hymns and a short reading from the scriptures, we acknowledge our dependence upon God's mercy and seek God's blessing on the day ahead. We might bless ourselves with holy water at Morning Prayer. We seal our prayer with the Lord's Prayer and the sign of peace. At Evening Prayer (also called vespers), the church gives thanks for the day's joys and sorrows and begs for God's continuing protection. We might begin with a service of candle lighting. We might also burn incense and sing Psalm 141: "My prayers rise like incense." We seal our prayer with the Lord's Prayer and the sign of peace.

Ideally, Morning and Evening Prayer are celebrated in common, but individuals are encouraged to mark the beginning and end of each day with prayer even if they cannot gather with others. At its heart, the Liturgy of the Hours calls us to a simple and repeated pattern of prayer, prayer that readily springs to our lips because it is already rooted deep in our hearts.

65

Stations of the Cross

There is something in us that moves us to visit the scene where an important event occurred. Visitors flock to the Ford Theater to stand where President Lincoln was assassinated; mourners visit the site of the Oklahoma City bombing; Elvis admirers tour Graceland. So it was for the early Christians who greatly desired to journey to Jerusalem and to see with their own eyes the places where Jesus lived, suffered and died. The traditional sites of the Lord's passion soon became popular stopping places; even today the Via Dolorosa is included in most pilgrims' itineraries.

Because not everyone was able to visit Jerusalem, pilgrims brought back stories and images of what they had seen for those who remained at home. Eventually shrines that focused on the passion and death of the Lord appeared all over Europe. In the fourteenth and fifteenth centuries, increased emphasis on the suffering of the Messiah, coupled with the fervor of the Franciscan friars, led to widespread acceptance of a devotion that traced the footsteps of Jesus from his trial to his tomb.

But it was more than curiosity that caused this devotion to flourish. Prayers that emphasized Jesus' obedience unto death, sorrow for sin, and God's abiding love and mercy were at the heart of it. Although the reforms of the Second Vatican Council placed greater emphasis on the Sunday Mass, the stations of the cross are still a valuable resource for prayer, especially during Lent, with its twofold emphasis on baptismal renewal and penitential acts.

Essential to this devotion, whether prayed by an individual or a group, is meditation on the passion of the Lord in spoken and sung prayer, and movement from one station to the next. Ideally, everyone walks in procession to each station, uniting ourselves in our bodies to the Lord's passion and death.

The number of stations has varied widely over the centuries. Recent revisions have omitted stations not included in the scriptures, and added stations that are, such as Jesus praying in the Garden of Olives, the denial of Jesus by Peter and Jesus' promise to the good thief. Frequently, a fifteenth station depicting the resurrection of Jesus is added to illustrate the fullness of the paschal mystery.

66

The Altar I

The word "altar" derives from the Latin *altare* (from *adolere* – burn), and came to be used in the early Christian church to designate the table on which was placed the bread and wine for eucharist. The Greek language used the word *thysiasterion* (table of sacrifice) to designate an altar. Paul speaks of the "table of the Lord" (1 Corinthians 10:21), and it is at a table that Jesus foretells his death, giving us the sacrificial gift that we will celebrate in his memory until we assemble at the banquet in heaven.

The altar, then, is a symbol of Christ in the midst of the assembly of believers, a table dedicated for both the sacrifice and the paschal banquet.

The altar was a simple free-standing table for the first few centuries of Christian worship, but it was soon affected by changing styles in church architecture and a changing theology of Christian worship. Ornate architectural detail, a more elaborate liturgy performed largely by the clergy and the placing of the altar on the rear wall of the apse meant that the altar was no longer the table of the assembly. It was primarily the resting place for the bread and wine for eucharist, the missal, candles, prayer cards, flowers and, later, the tabernacle.

The Second Vatican Council (1962 – 1965) revised the norms relating to the altar and used the earliest tradition of the church as its guide. Following this lead, the United States Bishops' Committee on the Liturgy wrote: "The altar, the holy table, should be the most noble, the most beautifully designed and constructed table the community can provide. It is the common table of the assembly, a symbol of the Lord. . . .

standing free, approachable from every side." (*Environment and Art in Catholic Worship*, #71)

The altar must be a piece of furniture of such beauty that it honors the holy action that occurs there, of such stature that it is worthy of the mystery celebrated there, of such eloquent simplicity that it invites the people of God to participate in a most extraordinary gift of sacrificial love. The altar stands as a worthy symbol of Christ and a holy table where God's people are nourished for their pilgrimage.

67

The Altar II

Have you ever noticed the priest kiss the altar at the beginning and end of Mass? This graceful act highlights the significance of the altar as a central symbol of our worship life.

Apart from the introduction of the use of the vernacular at Mass, the change in the location of the altar — away from the back wall of the church and into the midst of the assembly — is probably the most obvious effect of the Second Vatican Council. This change allowed people to gather more easily around the altar. Two related changes were also mandated by the Council. In the pre–Vatican II liturgy, because the priest alone performed most of the liturgical functions, a long altar was needed so that the two readings could be proclaimed from opposite ends of the altar while remaining separate from the eucharistic action, which took place in the center of the altar. Such an elongated table is no longer necessary. Secondly, because communion should be given from the sacrifice just enacted on the altar, the tabernacle was removed from the main altar. This maintains the integrity of both altar and tabernacle as sites of Christ's presence in the church. We have grown in our awareness of Christ's presence in the gathered assembly, in the proclamation of the word, in the person of the priest and in the eucharistic elements. We have been less attentive to the symbolic significance of the altar itself.

The Rite of Dedication of an Altar (which most often takes place during the dedication of the church in which the altar is located) gives us a glimpse of the significance of this symbol. In that rite, the altar is sprinkled with water, anointed with chrism and incensed by the bishop in a pattern much like our initiation rituals. It is then clothed with an altar cloth and adorned with lighted candles. These rituals leave no doubt that the altar is "the midpoint between heaven and earth." With the ancient images of Abraham's altar of sacrifice and the table of the Last Supper firmly rooted in our tradition, we encircle our parish altar, confident that God is present in our midst.

The Ambo

The word *ambo* derives from the Greek verb *anabainein* ("to go up") and was the name given to the elevated platform from which the scriptures were proclaimed in the large churches of the early Middle Ages. In smaller churches of the time, the priest and lector stood at the altar rail; only the bishop stood at the chair (the cathedra) for proclaiming and preaching. A later development saw elaborate, elevated pulpits attached to church pillars for better visibility and audibility. The liturgical reforms of the Second Vatican Council (1962 – 1965) called for the location of the ambo to be a natural focal point for the assembly during the liturgy of the word.

The ambo is a place for the act of proclamation. By its form and appearance it honors Christ present in the word, and hence evokes reverence and attentiveness when the word is sung or spoken from it. Here is the place for the proclamation of the scripture readings, the leading of the singing of psalms, for preaching God's word and perhaps for leading prayers of intercession. All other announcements and speeches are to be made elsewhere.

The ambo should be beautifully designed and carefully proportioned to suit its function — not as a shrine for the lectionary, but as a cradle for the word that embodies the story of our salvation, the mystery of the word made flesh among us.

The Chair

The ancient Latin word *cathedra,* used to designate the chair of a high-ranking civic official, was adopted by the early Christian church to refer to the cathedra or chair of the bishop. It was from the cathedra that the bishop presided at the liturgy and preached on the scriptures. Other chairs *(sedilia)* for attending priests and deacons were placed to the side. Later developments of church architecture saw the cathedra of the bishop elevated on a podium, and more throne-like in design. As parishes developed in the fourth century, a less ornate chair was used in the local church by the priest. The presider's or presidential chair soon became superfluous as the priest stood at the altar for most of the liturgical action.

The liturgical reform of this century has sought to recover the function of the chair of the presider. The materials and design of the chair should identify it as part of the particular place of worship. Its style should speak of the ministry of presiding, not of remoteness or prestige. Since we now have a fuller understanding of Christ's presence in the assembly of all the faithful, the presider's chair cannot signify privilege, but rather a sense of leadership in prayer, as well as the dignity and service that are inherent in Christian ministry.

From this chair, the presider calls the people of God to prayer, joins them in attentiveness to the word, keeps with them moments of silence, leads them in petitions of forgiveness, invites them to profess their faith, lifts up their intercessions for every need and sends them forth with God's blessing. And although rarely done by anyone other than a bishop, the rubrics allow preaching from the chair, too.

70

The Font

Baptism is one of the most revered and significant actions of the church. It is clearly rooted in Jesus' own baptism by John and grounded in the theology of Paul: "Do you not know that all of us who were baptized into Christ Jesus were baptized into his death? Therefore we have been buried with him by baptism into death, so that, just as Christ was raised from the dead by the glory of the Father, we too might walk in newness of life." (Romans 6:1–4)

The earliest evidence of special places for baptism is in a third-centruy house church in what is now Syria. In the fourth century, buildings called *baptistries* were provided for baptism. The container or *font* was large enough for an adult to be baptized by immersion. (To baptize means "to dip." "Immersion" means that the one being baptized stands or kneels in inches or feet of water while copious amounts of water are poured over his or her body.) It is unlikely that these early fonts were large

enough for submersion, that is, the whole body going under the surface of the water. Eventually, as infant baptism became the norm, the font became smaller and moved from the baptistry into the church.

With the revised rites for the celebration of baptism for infants (1969) and adults (1972 and 1988), and the earlier reform and restoration of the Easter Vigil (1951), the font is regaining its place.

Baptism is celebrated at the threshold of the life of faith, so it is appropriate for the font to be near the entrance of the church in an atrium or chapel. This would provide ample space for funeral processions to pause beside the font for the blessing of the casket. The design and scale of the font must clearly reflect the significance that the church attaches to initiation, to the mystery of incorporation into the eternal life of Christ that it celebrates.

The sign of baptism, however, is not the font, but the water in it. The abundant water speaks of the generous, life-giving grace of Christ poured over and into those who are "called by name" to put on the new life of Christ. The church, acting in Jesus' name, must show by its gestures and symbols fullness of hospitality toward all those initiated.

The font is the place for memorable rituals marking births and deaths, and the blessings of many spiritual journeys. The water of this font calls all who enter it, or touch it or are blessed by it, into that transformation whereby "we are alive for God in Christ Jesus" (Romans 6:11).

71

The Ambry

The word *ambry* is derived from the Latin *armarium* (cupboard or chest) and signifies the place where the vessels of oil used in celebrating sacraments are kept. These oils are blessed by the bishop at the Mass of Chrism celebrated during Holy Week and are brought to each parish church for the various rites of anointing. The three oils signify the universal charisms of the church for initiating (oil of catechumens), healing (oil of the sick) and consecrating (chrism).

As early as the sixth century, ambries were used to hold consecrated communion bread as well as the oils, and were often located in the base of the altar. By the thirteenth century, separate locked ambries were used for the eucharist only. This was an accepted practice by the sixteenth century, when this separate container was called a tabernacle. In the meantime, smaller amounts of the oils were stored in the sacristy, or in a simple wall niche or recessed cupboard known as an ambry.

As with all other vessels used in the liturgy today, the vessels for the oils should be of a quality and design that speak of the importance of the ritual actions. The vessels should hold an ample supply of the oils, thus symbolizing the generosity of God's gift. The gestures of anointing can then be performed with similar generosity of touch. The display of beautiful vessels reminds the community of the reverence it gives to its members as they are welcomed in baptism, confirmed in the spirit and anointed in their illness. To be anointed is to participate in an ancient biblical and ecclesial rite of blessing, and to enter into the mission of Jesus Christ, the anointed one of God.

72

The Chapel for the Tabernacle

In early Christian tradition, the practice of reserving the consecrated bread after the liturgy was to provide communion for those who were sick and unable to join the community at the Lord's table. In communities where was no daily Mass, the eucharist was also reserved for daily communion.

In some places, the laity were allowed to take the eucharist home with them. Eventually, the clergy reserved the eucharist, first in their houses, then in the sacristies. These sacristies were more like chapels. Eventually, the eucharist was reserved in a container near the altar — sometimes hanging above it in a vessel shaped like a dove!

The container used to hold the eucharistic bread (the consecrated wine was seldom reserved, even as now) was of various styles, and came to be known as the *tabernacle*. In the twelfth and thirteenth centuries, this tabernacle was located in a special chapel to accommodate the developing devotional practice of adoration. By the sixteenth century, in most places, the tabernacle became part of the main altar, where it was given prominence by architectural detail and liturgical reverence. In the liturgical reforms initiated by the Second Vatican Council, the church chose to return to the earlier practice of separating the tabernacle from the altar.

Various Roman documents from 1964 to 1983 show a strong preference for a distinct and distinguished chapel for the tabernacle. The 1983 Code of Canon Law states that the place where the tabernacle is housed must be "prominent, conspicuous, beautifully decorated and suited for prayer."

This chapel should accommodate the postures of prayer: sitting, kneeling, genuflecting. The tabernacle may be placed on a pillar or shelf, not normally on an altar. It may be recessed in the wall or suspended

from the ceiling. In all cases, it is to be secure and opaque. An oil lamp or candle should burn continuously near the tabernacle.

The chapel might be located next to the reconciliation chapel to provide the penitent with a place for prayer. If possible, it should be accessible even when the rest of the church building is occupied or otherwise unavailable.

This chapel is not intended to hide the tabernacle or diminish the importance of adoration; it is to provide appropriate honor for the reserved eucharist. When something is important to us, we make room for it, we create a shrine. When someone is important to us, we dedicate a space in our hearts and in our homes, both figuratively and literally, a private space for that one alone. This is the reasoning behind a chapel for the tabernacle.

73

The Tabernacle

The word *tabernacle* derives from the Latin *tabernaculum* (tent), and recalls the Jewish "meeting tent," which housed the ark of the covenant and thus embodied the presence of God among the people. In Catholic churches today, the tabernacle houses communion bread that has been consecrated at the liturgy. The practice of reserving the eucharist dates back in some places to the earliest days. In the second century, a small amount of consecrated communion bread was placed in an ambry or a pyx, often shaped like a casket or a dove. This vessel was small enough to be carried to the homes of those who were unable to attend the community's eucharist. This was the only reason for reservation. Devotion to the reserved eucharist grew during the Middle Ages when the reception of communion declined. By the sixteenth century, the custom of a fixed container for the reserved eucharist — the tabernacle as part of the main altar — was in place; in 1614 it became prescribed practice for most places.

The normative guidelines of the church today indicate that the tabernacle be placed elsewhere than on an altar, and never on the altar used for the liturgy. An appropriate setting would be on a pillar, in a wall niche, or especially, in a chapel set apart from the main assembly area. (The chapel is the clear preference of Roman liturgical law.) Such a setting should also provide for the private devotion of the faithful. The tabernacle in its modern setting still recalls the ancient image of a house for the divine presence, and reminds the assembly of those in the parish who are confined to their households, waiting for the ministry of those who have celebrated the eucharist.

The tabernacle is made of noble materials, giving it a quiet dignity as the symbol of an ever-present God. A lamp burns nearby in silent witness of this mystery.

74

The Reconciliation Chapel

The place where the sacrament of reconciliation is to be celebrated as part of the faith life of the community remains an unsettled issue. Some of us recall the confessional, the "box," with its hard kneeler, dim light (if any), hushed tones and cramped quarters. There was an obvious connection between physical austerity, the discomfort of being in the box and the darkness of the sins to be confessed or the harshness of the penance to be assigned.

The reform of the Second Vatican Council (1962–1965) has helped us come to a greater awareness of the wonderful gift of God's forgiving love as the primary focus of the sacrament. As are all the sacraments, reconciliation is communal in nature; it is more than an act of confession of personal peccadilloes. It is reconciliation with our sisters and brothers who are the church, as well as reconciliation with God. The celebrating of this sacrament, which returns us to the embrace of the church "through the merits of the Lord Jesus and power of Holy Spirit," requires a special place.

Although there is no liturgical norm requiring a separate room for reconciliation, or specifying guidelines for its design, there are some excellent opinions in the current literature on the environment for worship that deserve serious consideration. In *Shaping a House for the Church,* Marchita

Mauck writes, "The integrity and holiness of the ritual of penance demands an honored place reserved for it alone." This means that the place for reconciliation is dedicated to that sole purpose. The place does not also serve as a storage room, extra sacristy or a cry-room. It is properly a chapel, a place for worship, for liturgy; it is not a counseling room or therapist's office. In keeping with our understanding of the sacrament of reconciliation as an experience of conversion and of reclaiming our baptismal identity, the chapel for reconciliation could be located in relationship to the baptismal font. Since reconciliation returns us to the common table, the eucharistic gathering, it is appropriate for the reconciliation chapel to open into the main worship area. As Mauck points out, "reconciliation is about re-entry and re-union as church."

The design of the reconciliation chapel should take into account the options that the rite intends: face-to-face confession or anonymity; sitting, kneeling or standing as the penitent chooses. The placement and material of a partition or screen, sacred art, acoustical privacy and the proper lighting and ventilation are all important elements. This is a holy place; we are never more vulnerable than when we approach this sacrament, and never more conscious of God's love than when we stand forgiven.

75

The Ringing of Bells

The ringing of bells has been associated with Christian worship for centuries. It is said that people never forget the unique sound of their own parish bells no matter how long they are away. Bells in church buildings were often given names, for example, "Gabriel bells," in honor of the angel Gabriel, the messenger of good news.

The dedication of church bells, referred to as the "baptism of a bell," was an elaborate ceremony, using holy water, blessed oil and prayers of invocation. Blessed bells were regarded as a sacramental. The first known use of bells in churches was by a bishop named Paulinus in the year 400. By the Middle Ages, the ringing of bells had become an elaborate ritual rich with symbolism: the "sacrament bell" was rung to get people's attention before the sermon (it's not known if this was as a warning or as a welcome!), the "Ave bells" were rung during devotions to Mary at certain times of the day and the "passing bells" solemnly tolled at funerals.

One of the other reasons for ringing bells during the liturgy was to announce the elevation of the host and of the chalice. An architectural feature of churches for many years was the separation of the sanctuary from the main assembly area by large, ornate partitions known as rood screens. (It was thought that only the clergy and choir could watch the sacred actions. Even the choir wasn't always allowed to observe the elevation, and a curtain was drawn around the altar and priest at this time.) Many of us remember the remnant of the rood screen, the altar rail. On the other side of the rood screen, the congregation involved itself in private devotions and prayers such as the rosary, since they were not active participants in the action of the liturgy. The bells were rung by servers to announce that something important was happening, so that the people could participate by ear, if not by eye. Often chalices were adorned with small bells so that the movement up and down would attract people's attention.

But now, long after the rood screens have disappeared, with the altar in the midst of the assembly and everyone able to see the actions of the liturgy and encouraged to join in the dialogue and acclamations of the eucharistic prayer, the bells are no longer necessary at this point in the Mass.

The ringing of outside bells is a marvelous and traditional way to call people to worship, to enhance liturgical processions or to announce the times of morning and evening prayer. Even when silent, bells evoke a certain attention to the place they adorn as they wait to summon the community to prayer.

Suggested Schedule Sunday by Sunday

The chart below offers one possible plan or outline for an entire year's worth of articles. It begins with the First Sunday of Advent. The final order will vary depending on the calendar cycle for a particular year. The inserts listed in italics are not time-specific and may be used on other dates, or even repeated if needed.

1. Advent (A Sense of the Season)
2. Eternity's Clock and Crown
3. Nuestra Señora de Guadalupe (December 12)
4. Gospel of the Year (Matthew/Mark/Luke)
5. Christmas (A Sense of the Season)
    or The Paradise Tree
6. Bless Your Door on Epiphany
7. Ordinary Time: Winter (A Sense of the Season)
8. Martin Luther King Day
    (Third Monday in January)
9. *The Catechumenate*
10. Saint Blase (February 3)
11. *Q&A: Who's Who (Who are the catechumens?)*
12. *Dismissal of Catechumens*
13. *Q&A: Candidates in Church
    (Who are the candidates?)*
14. Lenten Fast and Abstinence:
    An Invitation to Awareness
15. Lent (A Sense of the Season)
16. Rite of Election
17. Scrutinies
18. Stations of the Cross
19. This Is the Night
    or Triduum (A Sense of the Season)
20. Eastertime (A Sense of the Season)
    or The Pillar of Fire
21. *Finding Our Place*
22. *We Bow Before You*
23. *Renewing Baptism*
24. *The Church's Daily Prayer*
25. The Ascension of the Lord
26. Mission and Mystagogy
27. Ordinary Time: Summer (A Sense of the Season)
28. Charles Lwanga and Companions (June 3)
29. Apostles Peter and Paul (June 29)
30. Blessed Kateri Tekakwitha (July 14)
31. *Q&A: What to Read
    (How are the readings chosen?)*
32. *Sing Psalms*
33. *Silence*
34. *The Collection
    or The Altar II*
35. *Always Thanksgiving*
36. *Communion from the Cup*
37. *Communion Song*
38. Celebrating the Human Body
    (August 15)
39. *Going to a Wedding*
40. Ordinary Time: Autumn
    (A Sense of the Season)
41. The Triumph of the Cross (September 14)
42. *One of the Q&A from Sunday Eucharist section:
    Inclusive Language, More than Once,
    Stipends*
43. *Anointing of the Sick I
    or Communion Call*
44. *Anointing of the Sick II
    or Communion of the Dying*
45. *Q&A: Another Wedding
    (What is convalidation?)*
46. *Q&A: No Obligation
    (Why is the obligation waived?)*
47. *Rite of Acceptance*
48. All Saints' Day (November 1)
    or All Souls' (November 2)
    or Andrew Dung-Lac and Companions
    (November 24)
49. *Order of Christian Funerals I: The Vigil*
50. *Order of Christian Funerals II:
    The Funeral Liturgy*
51. *Order of Christian Funerals III:
    The Rite of Committal*
52. *Concerns about Funerals*

The remaining articles from this volume may be rotated into the above outline as the needs and circumstances of the parish dictate.

Article Title	For Whom/Publication	Date Used
Advent (A Sense of the Season)		
All Saints' Day		
All Souls'		
The Altar I		
The Altar II		
Always Thanksgiving		
The Ambo		
The Ambry		
Andrew Dung-Lac and Companions		
Anointing of the Sick I		
Anointing of the Sick II		
Apostles Peter and Paul		
The Ascension of the Lord		
Bless Your Door on Epiphany		
Blessed Kateri Tekakwitha		
The Catechumenate		
Celebrating the Human Body		
The Chair		
The Chapel for the Tabernacle		
Charles Lwanga and Companions		
Christmas (A Sense of the Season)		
The Church's Daily Prayer		
The Collection		
Communion Call		
Communion from the Cup		
Communion of the Dying		
Communion Song		
Concerns about Funerals		
Dismissal of Catechumens		
Eastertime (A Sense of the Season)		
Eternity's Clock and Crown		
Finding Our Place		
The Font		
Going to a Wedding		
The Gospel of John		
The Gospel of Luke		
The Gospel of Mark		
The Gospel of Matthew		

Article Title	For Whom/Publication	Date Used
Lent (A Sense of the Season)		
Lenten Fast and Abstinence: Invitation to Awareness		
Martin Luther King Day		
Mission and Mystagogy		
Nuestra Señora de Guadalupe		
Order of Christian Funerals I: The Vigil		
Order of Christian Funerals II: The Funeral Liturgy		
Order of Christian Funerals III: The Rite of Committal		
Ordinary Time: Autumn (A Sense of the Season)		
Ordinary Time: Summer (A Sense of the Season)		
Ordinary Time: Winter (A Sense of the Season)		
The Paradise Tree		
Period of Evangelization		
The Pillar of Fire		
Q&A: Another Wedding		
Q&A: Candidates in Church		
Q&A: Inclusive Language		
Q&A: More than Once		
Q&A: No Obligation		
Q&A: Stipends		
Q&A: What to Read		
Q&A: Who's Who		
The Reconciliation Chapel		
Renewing Baptism		
The Ringing of Bells		
Rite of Acceptance		
Rite of Election		
Saint Blase Blessing		
Silence		
Sing Psalms		
Scrutinies		
Stations of the Cross		
The Tabernacle		
This Is the Night		
Triduum (A Sense of the Season)		
Triumph of the Cross		
We Bow Before You		

CLIP NOTES FOR CHURCH BULLETINS • CD-ROM INFORMATION

HOW TO USE The CD on the inside back cover contains word processing files for both the text and artwork printed in this book. To explore this disk, insert the CD-ROM in your computer's CD-ROM drive. Change to the CD-ROM drive and "change directory" to the subdirectory named after the word processing program you use. There you will find text files named for the page numbers in this book. The artwork can be found in the TIFF (Tagged Image File Format) subdirectory.

MS-DOS/IBM-PC compatible formats are WordPerfect 5.1 and Microsoft Word 6.0. If you are using either of these programs, or an upgraded version, you may import or merge the text file you want into your own document. If you are using a different program, you will need to import a text file by having that program convert the file from WordPerfect or Word.

MACINTOSH formats included on the CD are WordPerfect 1.0, Microsoft Word 3.0 and Claris Works 4.0. Import these files directly into your software (if you are using one of these programs), or convert one of these files into your software format if you are using a different program.

ARTWORK is available as TIFF files. Each file (or piece of art) is named for its page number in this book. Please refer to page numbers for the file names you want.

LICENSE AND LIMITED WARRANTY As with the printed pages of this book, this CD-ROM is licensed for exclusive use by the original purchaser. Liturgy Training Publications warrants that the CD-ROM is free from defect in material and work-manship for a period of thirty days from the date of purchase. Defective CDs must be returned to LTP within this warranty period in order to be replaced at no charge. This program is provided "AS IS" and Liturgy Training Publications is in no way liable or responsible for any problems that may arise from its use. This statement shall be construed, interpreted and governed by the laws of the State of Illinois.

COPYRIGHT Except for adaptations of format, size and type fonts, no part of the text or artwork provided on the CD may be changed, deleted or altered in any fashion without the permission of Liturgy Training Publications. The copyright notice as found on each page must appear with each use.

FOR TECHNICAL ASSISTANCE CALL JERRY ALBER, 1-773-486-8970, x256